metamorphustice
stages of justice reform
™

metamorphustice™
stages of justice reform

MEGAN
FUCIARELLI

PALMETTO
PUBLISHING
Charleston, SC
www.PalmettoPublishing.com

Copyright © 2023 by Megan Fuciarelli

Paperback ISBN: 979-8-8229-3447-4
eBook ISBN: 979-8-8229-3448-1

To all who helped me within my own transformation… -Megan

Table of Contents

Foreword   i

Introduction   v

Section One
Foundational Principles of Social Justice Work

1. How do I transform social justice?   3
2. Guilt and politeness are the glue that hold prejudice and stigma in place.   7
3. Intentions ≠ Impact   17
4. We must intentionally include so as not to unintentionally exclude.   27
5. Seek to impact someone's heart, which will ultimately change their mind.   37
6. Every issue counts.   45
7. Growth occurs in discomfort.   53
8. Once you know better, do better!   61

Section Two
Components of JEDI (Justice, Equity, Diversity, Inclusion) Work

1. What is included within social justice transformation?   71
2. Diversity: Being SEEN   75

3. Inclusion: Being HEARD   83
4. Equity: Being WELCOMED   91
5. Justice: Being VALUED   101
6. What happens when one (or more) of these
    components are missing?   109

Section Three
Stages of Metamorphustice™

1. Why is social justice reform called
    metamorphustice™?   133
2. Stage 1: Oblivious   139
3. Stage 2: Defensive   149
4. Stage 3: Savior   159
5. Stage 4: Ally   169
6. Stage 5: Advocate   177
7. Stage 6: Co-Conspirator   185
8. Stage 7: CHANGEmaker   193

Section Four
Becoming Pollinators of Change

1. How can I transform as an individual?   209
2. How can I transform as a family member?   217
3. How can I transform as an educator?   223
4. How can I transform as a community member?   229
5. How can I transform as a leader?   235

Acknowledgements   241
About the Author   243

Foreword

The work of social justice is not new; however, over recent years, it has become more 'popular' across mainstream society. I have been in the social justice space, as an educator and now a business owner, for over 25 years. I did not always know about the struggles facing so many within our country, though. It was not until I went away to college that I was even exposed to people who were different than myself. I have gone through many stages of awareness and, over the last 25 years, have worked very hard to understand myself better. In turn, I have been able to help others understand themselves as well. This idea of understanding self before working to unite society is what launched US², my company focused on empowering individuals to be the CHANGE they wish to see in the world.

You will notice that the word CHANGE is in all capital letters. This is intentional and serves as an acronym within our company to align with our core values of Commitment, Heart-Focused, Accountable, Networking, Genuine, and Empowerment. Our company believes that by aligning everything we do to these values, we are able to instill CHANGE on a greater level – leading to long-lasting impact. I'd like to invite you to consider the importance of these attributes as well. Commitment speaks to the drive for CHANGE and not giving up. Aligning to the heart reminds us that people are human first. Accountability ensures that work doesn't 'fall between the cracks' when we get busy. Talking to one another and engaging in conversation keeps the conversation at the forefront. Being genuine encourages others to be authentic, and ultimately, psychologically safe. By empowering and uplifting others around us, we are creating a world of powerful, empathetic, and inspiring humans.

It is critical for us to look in the mirror before trying to 'change' or 'fix' anyone else. Once we understand our own baggage and the impact of our experiences, we can support others in doing similar work. This book has been on my heart and mind for years; however, with recent events in our society, the business has grown exponentially. I needed to make a decision about where to focus my energy – and I chose our clients. I have now decided that this book can start the transformation our society needs (and in a way that people can digest without defensiveness).

This is my personal message to all readers: You WILL make mistakes when it comes to social justice work. You WILL get defensive from time to time. You WILL reflect on previous conversations and have some

moments of 'yuck'. I know this sounds pessimistic –
it's not. It's realistic. We ALL have biases, and we ALL
have different experiences that impact how we see the
world and how others see us. We will not be able to
unite society until we humanize the concept of bias. I
hold the vision of a more united society – will you hold
the vision with me?

Introduction

An egg hatches into a caterpillar and then, after experiencing some of the world, morphs into a butterfly. Once becoming a butterfly, they are able to fly and explore the world around them – far beyond their reach as a caterpillar. As they explore, they pollinate flowers by drinking their nectar and transferring pollen. As humans, we are similar. As young children, we are innocent and there is so much potential for growth (similar to that of an egg). As we age, we start to confront our truths and vulnerabilities through self-reflection, which can be difficult, and sometimes sticky (similar to that of a chrysalis). And as we grow older, we are able to explore more and ultimately emerge as our true selves and share experiences (similar to that of a butterfly). Just as a butterfly becomes a pollinating agent, spreading pollen from one flower to the next, we too have the ability to spread impact with our actions, words, and commitment to social justice.

The transformation of a caterpillar to a butterfly is called metamorphosis. In this book, I will talk about the metamorphosis of justice, coined metamorphustice™.

As individuals, it is critical to treat social justice reform as a transformational process that continues in a cyclical pattern. As a society, if we don't truly transform how we see the world and how we interact with one another, we will continue to silence and ignore our fellow community members.

This book is meant to provoke internal dialogue, reflection, and provide actionable steps within an individual. Journal prompts are embedded within the text as well as real-world examples. While reflecting using the journal prompts, consider a separate journal dedicated to this work. Remember that there are no 'correct' answers; rather, it is honest answers (even if not favorable) that will help guide the transformational process of social justice reform. Once you have processed some of your own insights, I invite you to use some of the prompts as starting points for discussions with friends, family members, and/or colleagues. Examples are provided to create concrete context and inspire further personal reflections. As you encounter the examples, consider how they relate to your own experiences and/or observations.

The first section will identify and unpack foundational principles to consider. They help us evolve, challenge our biases, and inspire transformation. The second section will discuss the four Components of JEDI (Justice, Equity, Diversity, & Inclusion) work while identifying what is missing from each of these components when implemented in isolation. The third section will walk readers through the stages of justice reform, metamorphustice™. The final section will provide actionable steps on how to move forward in your own transformational process.

My own transformation of driving meaningful change has been an evolution much like that of a butterfly; marked by self-reflection, the embracing of uncomfortable moments, and the recognition that change begins with ourselves. This transformation is not without struggles – between self-doubt, saviorism, self-hatred, and anger. I am continuing to grow every day. I share this not to say that I have 'reached the pinnacle of transformation'. Instead, I share this to show the humanity in all of us. As I wrote this book, I had even more transformational moments and I hope that you can experience similar moments as well. Transformation is not a solitary endeavor but a collective movement. We must be willing to share our vulnerabilities, to confront our biases, to ask questions, and to challenge the status quo.

I will share more stories throughout, but please allow me to start here. I have multiple titles, but the most important to me is Mommy. My second most important is Daughter. All of us have multiple titles – some attached to work, some attached to family, and some attached to our own definitions of self. I do this work for my son and my unborn grandchildren. I do this work because ALL of us deserve to be heard, seen, welcomed, and valued. I do this work because I believe in the power of humanity and the impact that one person can make. I invite all of you to continue reading with the intention of being the CHANGE we need in the world.

Journal Prompts:

1. What is/are your personal core value(s)?

_____

_____

_____

_____

2. What are you most interested in learning more about?

_____

_____

_____

_____

3. During what stage of your life did/do you see the most transformation (childhood, early adulthood, later adulthood)?

_____

_____

_____

_____

4. What title(s) do you hold? What is/are most important to you?

_____

_____

_____

_____

5. Why did you choose to read this book?

_____

_____

_____

_____

6. How do you respond when you are disappointed with yourself? How can you practice grace with yourself while reading this book?

_____

_____

_____

_____

7. What will you do to best prepare yourself to be vulnerable and honest while reading this book?

_____

_____

_____

_____

SECTION ONE

Foundational Principles of Social Justice Work

UNDERSTAND SELF | UNITE SOCIETY

Consider
this question

'How do 'I transform
social justice?

In our lives, when we are taught about a new concept, we are first given definitions and the foundation for common understanding. This idea is no different when thinking about social justice work. In this first section, I will be sharing seven foundational principles that shape how we can make the strongest impact toward uniting society.

This common foundation provides clarity and alignment. If society is aligned with expectations, there is a stronger sense of understanding which leads to the ability to make a stronger impact. When we all speak the same language of equity, inclusion, and respect, it becomes easier to work together toward a common goal. For example, if an organization is committed to social justice efforts (i.e., equitable pay structures, accessible facilities, health insurance for all loved ones, regardless of gender identity), and that is discussed in initial onboarding meetings, new employees are aware immediately of what the organization stands for and what is important to the organization.

Common foundations also prevent misinterpretation. This misinterpretation can lead to misunderstandings, conflicts, or even the unintentional reinforcement of harmful stereotypes and/or biases. For example, if a community group is working to bring together a community with very different viewpoints and uses 'trigger words' such as privilege and/or fragility without defining the terms in ways that can be understood without defensiveness, the community group might actually further polarize the community. This can ultimately hinder communication and collaboration.

A common foundation amplifies the impact of collective efforts. By coming together as a collective, resources, knowledge, and experiences can be multiplied allowing actions to resonate more powerfully – fostering meaningful transformation. For example, in a school setting, by including all members of the school community (parents/guardians/caregivers, staff, students, and community members), there is power in numbers. Both students and adults have the opportunity to learn from others who may have different experiences.

Guilt and politeness are
the glue that hold prejudice
and stigma in place.

_____
_____
_____
_____
_____
_____
_____
_____
_____
_____
_____
_____
_____
_____
_____
_____
_____
_____
_____
_____
_____
_____
_____

Guilt is a strong emotion – and one that is infused throughout our lives in many ways. As a child, I was taught not to stare at people who were physically different from myself. This often went a step beyond staring, though. Even if I was curious and wanted to look, the assumption was that I was staring. Many of you might be able to relate to this. My parents and grandparents, who initially told me 'not to stare' meant well. But what they taught me is that curiosity is shameful and that asking questions can evoke negative feelings. Fast forward to conversations with my son. I have taught him from an early age to be curious and to ask questions. As much as we apologize in our family, we try not to equate that to guilt. We learn from our missteps and move forward – at least we try to.

The first Core Principle to consider is, "Guilt and politeness are the glue that hold prejudice and stigma in place." This can be further expanded to say "Guilt, shame, blame, and politeness…" As US[2] states, it is important to look inward at self before looking outward at society. Unfortunately, there is a lot of negative discourse surrounding social justice – whether it is out of blaming a specific group for the problems of today or simply ignoring topics. Both of these are damaging to the progress of our society. Let's start with defining some of these words, both from a historical and current day lens.

Guilt in the context of social justice has often been used as a tool to assign responsibility and demand accountability. The intention behind movements, such as the Civil Rights Movement, Black Lives Matter, and Women's Suffrage Movement, is to drive progress and justice; however, the weight of these movements, at times, has hindered constructive dialogue and collaborative efforts. For instance, in the aftermath of the Civil Rights Movement, many well-intentioned individuals grappled with guilt over past complacency or ignorance regarding racial discrimination. This guilt can serve as a catalyst for meaningful change, but it also can lead to defensiveness. This defensiveness can cause people to resist acknowledging their biases or privilege because doing so would mean accepting their role in perpetuating social injustices. Moreover, guilt can be paralyzing. Individuals who feel overwhelmed by guilt may become unsure of how to contribute constructively to change. This guilt often overshadows the positive potential of individual and collective action, stifling progress. Many argue that a level of guilt can be constructive, causing someone to reflect on their behaviors and shift future decisions. Although this may be true for some people, I do not recommend guilt as a tactic to address social justice transformation.

Shame also has deep historical roots in perpetuating prejudice and discrimination. Throughout history, marginalized groups have been subjected to societal shame, often reinforcing stereotypes and bias. For example, in the early 20th century, the eugenics movement used shame to stigmatize people with disabilities, advocating for their exclusion and even forced sterilization. Shame has been used as a means of control and oppression, forcing individuals to conform to societal norms, often at the expense of their own identities and well-being. Shame has also been wielded as a weapon to silence those who challenge the status quo. Activists, especially those from marginalized communities, are often shamed for their advocacy, labeled as 'troublemakers' or 'agitators'. The history of shame has created barriers to open discourse. With the "Don't Ask, Don't Tell" policy that was in place for over 17 years, military personnel who identified as non-heterosexual were discharged from serving. A variation of this policy was later implemented: "Don't Ask, Don't Tell; Don't Pursue, Don't Harass". The inclusion of this addendum to the policy clearly shows that there were issues with harassment; however, instead of eliminating the policy, it was simply modified. Military personnel who were in a relationship with someone of the opposite gender were able to share photos and speak of their relationship; while those who were in a relationship with someone outside of hetero-normative culture were shamed and excluded. Many military personnel chose to 'cloak' their identity due to this policy. The idea of 'cloaking' is similar to the concept of masking; someone who has the ability to hide a particular identity from society and choose who to share that with is able to 'cloak' their identity. For example, someone might hide aspects of themselves from certain people in their lives while sharing those same aspects with different people. In addition to this example regarding sexuality, body image and weight have been long associated with shame as well. Within our society, if individuals do not conform to conventional beauty and/or body standards, they are often shamed, which leads to self-esteem issues. When talking about shame, US[2] also encourages the cessation of the word 'should'. Should, in and of itself, evokes shame, which can lead to self-deprecating behaviors and lead to a toxic environment where individuals are unwilling to be authentic due to a fear of public humiliation.

Blame has been a prevalent force in the social justice landscape, often serving as a shortcut to identifying responsibility for societal issues. Blaming specific groups or individuals for societal problems has been a common strategy throughout history. Consider, for instance, the blame often placed on immigrants for economic challenges, or the blame assigned to different racial or religious groups. Blame directs attention away from the systemic factors that underlie these challenges and creates scapegoats. It prevents us from working collaboratively to address systemic issues and fosters a sense of hostility and division among communities. Blame reinforces the notion of 'otherness' and 'enemy', which can make it challenging to find common ground or engage in meaningful dialogue. Instead of addressing the root causes of issues, societies become mired in finger-pointing and divisive rhetoric. Blame has become the main culprit in society's divisiveness. We are more polarized today than ever. Until we stop blaming one another, we will not be able to come together.

Politeness is not the same as respect. For the purposes of this statement, politeness is equated to what we used to call being 'politically correct'. We have moved away from using the phrase 'politically correct' – probably because of how openly divisive leaders have become. The phrase 'politically correct' basically means that we avoid controversial topics (and almost every topic can be controversial). It is important to not avoid difficult topics. At the same time, when we do get into discussions where people might have a difference of opinion, we must respect one another at all times. Listening to someone does not mean that you agree with them. If we continue to ignore topics because we are afraid of how the other person will respond, we are doing nothing to break down the prejudice and stigma that exists in our society. And, by not breaking these barriers down, we are actually continuing to uplift the biases that influence our world.

The historical use of guilt, shame, blame, and politeness have all contributed to the polarization of society in several profound ways. These tactics have often been wielded as weapons in ideological battles, reinforcing an 'us vs. them' mentality. More specifically, in politics, we are seeing this cause a divide that hinders bipartisan efforts to create effective reform policies. In education, we are seeing communities losing trust in their school systems due to a disconnect in what is 'appropriate' to be taught in schools.

Ultimately, as individuals, we need to be able to embrace every aspect of who we are and humanize who others are while leaning into respectful discourse that doesn't avoid controversial topics. When you are fairly new within your transformational process of metamorphustice™, you will likely experience some form of guilt, shame, and/or blame – and you will likely want to avoid certain conversations. This is often stemming from a lack of understanding, experiences to draw from, and/or lack of skills to be able to lean into a difficult conversation. The first step in this process is to reflect on how you are feeling and process the journal prompts within this book. Allow yourself to feel whatever it is that you are feeling, journal about it, reflect on where this belief may be originating from, and then grow your skillset.

There are quite a few activities that you can consider when looking to overcome guilt, shame, blame, and politeness:

> List the identities you hold and what you are proud of about your specific identities. Examples of identities would be race, gender, sexuality,

religion, dis/ability status, etc. This activity is most beneficial if you can say you are proud of ALL your identities without hesitation. It is important to note that pride in self is not the same as feeling superior compared to someone else.

> When you find yourself blaming someone else, ask yourself, "What have I done to contribute to this problem?" and "What can I do to contribute to the solution?"

> Ask questions – even when it is uncomfortable.

> Ask permission before asking a question that society might view as 'inappropriate'.

Journal Prompts:

1. Reflect on the polarization of our society. How does blame, shame, guilt, and/or politeness contribute to this polarization?

   _____

   _____

   _____

   _____

2. What strategies can be employed to shift the focus from blame to a more constructive approach when addressing complex social challenges related to divisive topics?

   _____

   _____

   _____

   _____

3. Reflect on a time when you witnessed or experienced shame related to social justice issues. How did this impact others around you?

   _____

   _____

   _____

   _____

4. Have you ever felt guilt in the context of social justice issues? What triggered this feeling and how did you respond?

_____

_____

_____

_____

5. When was the last time you 'held your tongue' or stayed silent although you wanted to ask a question because you were afraid of how the other person might receive your question and/or statement?

_____

_____

_____

_____

6. What have you 'cloaked' about yourself because you were worried about how others might perceive you?

_____

_____

_____

_____

7. How does mass media (social media, news outlets, etc.) play into the concept of shame and blame perpetuating biases?

_____

_____

_____

_____

What does
this statement mean
to you?

Intentions ≠ Impact

_____
_____
_____
_____
_____
_____
_____
_____
_____
_____
_____
_____
_____
_____
_____
_____
_____
_____
_____
_____
_____
_____
_____
_____

Play along with me for a minute… You are in the middle of a conversation and things are going great. The other person is engaged and seems genuinely invested in the conversation. And then, after a statement you make, the person seems to completely shift their mannerisms. You wonder, 'What did I say?" or maybe you start to wonder if you have something in your teeth. When, in actuality, you might have spoken a microaggressive statement – without even realizing it. A microaggression is defined as a statement and/or behavior said, or done, by an individual that minimizes, invalidates, or harms another person, or group of people, based on identity. Maybe you even gave what you considered a compliment such as, "You speak so well!" or invalidated the experiences of an entire group of people by saying, "I don't see color – I treat everyone the same!" Both of these statements, albeit well-intentioned, are microaggressions. I myself have both said and heard microaggressions. Microaggressions stem from stereotypes that we have heard within society and the only way to address them is to talk openly (as Core Principle #1 shares) and to acknowledge that intentions do not always equal impact (Core Principle #2).

We all like to believe that our intentions are pure and noble. When we set out to make a positive difference or to support a cause we care about, our intentions are often grounded in care and compassion. We genuinely want to help, uplift, and bring about positive change in the lives of others. We will talk more about this when defining the seven stages of metamor- phustice™. However, the paradox lies in the fact that having good intentions does not guarantee positive outcomes. Our actions and words can have unintend- ed consequences, sometimes leading to hurt, misun- derstanding, or even exacerbating the very issues we sought to address. Why does this happen? It happens because our intentions, no matter how well-meaning, are not the sole determinants of our impact. Intentions exist within the realm of our minds, shaped by our perspectives, values, and worldviews. And impact is determined in the same way – by the person receiving the message.

At times, we recognize almost immediately that we said or did something harmful (these are known as 'open mouth, insert foot' moments). Other times, and more often, we don't even understand the impact of what we say on someone else. I believe that most people have the best of intentions most of the time – at least from their lens. People don't typically wake up in the morning thinking about how much harm they are going to do in that day – and getting excited by it. Saying this, though, does not excuse the harm that can be caused. If we embrace the idea that intentions do not equal impact and humanize that all of us will make mistakes, we can have more impactful conversations leading to a more united society.

Another point to address within this Core Principle of "Intentions ≠ Impact" is that it is only the person impacted that can share how they were impacted. For example, if someone says they were harmed by something you said, you don't have the right to tell them they can't be hurt because that wasn't your intention. Oftentimes, people will minimize the hurt they caused someone else due to shame they have for hurting someone. As shared previously, most people don't WANT to hurt others – and it still happens. Instead of providing excuses of why you didn't mean something the way the person received it, say, "Thank you for sharing that with me. I didn't see it from your perspective. Now that I know, I will be more mindful in the future." Genuine listening and reflection are critical to be able to bridge the gap between intentions and impact.

Let's provide a few examples of how intentions do not always align with impact before moving forward with the discussion around perspective and how that impacts someone's reality. Imagine you are speaking to someone about a horrible day you had, and they instantly jump in to offer unsolicited advice. The intention behind this is to be helpful and offer solutions; however, the impact may be the feeling of being dismissed or not heard. In this situation, we recommend asking, "How can I best support you right now?" Sometimes, we simply want someone to listen (and maybe even join the sharing of disappointment); other times, we may want advice. By asking the best way to support someone and/or the goal of the conversation beforehand will often support with aligning the intentions with the impact.

Another example involves parenting. I have seen this both in my current role as a mother and previously in my role as a daughter. My parents encouraged me to excel – to the point that if I got a B, I was asked why it wasn't an A. They had the best of intentions. They knew that grades would help me secure my place in a prominent college and, ultimately, support me with finding a job that paid well (which was the standard for a 'good job' growing up). What I grew up thinking from that was that if I wasn't 'perfect', I wasn't good enough… This was definitely NOT my parents' intentions; nor is it mine when I find myself pushing my son to excel academically. Please know that I believe strongly in the power of learning and focus a lot of energy on our educational system; I also believe that the pressure often placed on students leads to high levels of stress and/or anxiety. Instead of striving for 100%, I invite you to ask the questions, "Are you proud of how you did? Why/Why not? What will you do in the future to maintain your pride in self and/or increase your pride in self?" These questions allow the person to self-disclose their opinion – which leads to a stronger alignment between intentions and impact.

Another example involves the workplace. Imagine being very proud of the work your team is doing to become more inclusive (i.e., increased visible diversity among the workforce, decreased gap between pay across genders, increased tenure among all identities). You believe some of the best ways to continue this work is to showcase your efforts and speak specifically to employees that had been marginalized in the past within your company. You prepare a report to share with the company highlighting your conversations and the growth that has occurred within the company. While your intention was to showcase the great work being done, some of the employees that you spoke to felt targeted and were uncomfortable being the 'voice' of all people within their identity. Others in the company also felt that the report highlighting only certain attributes seemed more like a 'check box' than a genuine value within the company. In order to address this scenario, it is important to consistently align with your business/organizational values and invite everyone to share their story – not just a selected group.

All of these examples provide different perspectives on the same situation. Our own experiences impact how we see the world around us – which makes the Core Principle of intentions not equaling impact even more difficult to discern at times. There are unlimited ways to see and/or experience an event. To understand this better, we must acknowledge that people often make decisions and act based on what they know, believe, and/or experience – leading to the perception of an action/behavior. Peoples' perceptions often become their reality (impact) unless more communication occurs. Our intentions are shaped by our perspectives, values, and worldviews. These two (intentions and impact) can misalign, causing harm.

Common examples of intentions not aligning with impact are microaggressions. As mentioned earlier in this chapter, microaggressions are often committed by people who genuinely have the best of intentions. Whether they are giving what they view as a compliment (microinsult) or whether they are telling what they view as a joke (microinvalidation), the impact is often negative. Recognizing microaggressions and their potential impact is a crucial step in bridging the gap between intentions and outcomes. It requires self-awareness and empathy and involves being open to feedback and willing to learn from the experience of others. When we acknowledge that even well-intentioned actions and words can contain microaggressions, we have an opportunity to learn and evolve. We must engage in open and compassionate dialogue by actively listening to those affected by microaggressions, asking for their perspective, and demonstrating a willingness to understand and empathize.

The second Core Principle reminds us that the transformation of social justice can be fraught with complexities and misunderstandings. We must be able to recognize different perspectives, hold ourselves accountable for our actions that cause harm (even when well-intentioned), and learn from those around us. By embracing the wisdom that intentions alone do not guarantee impact and acknowledging the presence of microaggressions, we can forge a more compassionate and understanding path forward.

There are quite a few activities that you can consider when looking to align intentions with impact:

> Preface conversations (or step back mid-conversation) with your intention and ask the other person to share if the intention is not being received.
> If someone shares that you said a microaggression, ask for clarity (being mindful of tone), thank them for sharing their perspective with you, and commit to learning for future conversations (with others, not just the person you are speaking to).
> Be mindful of levels of defensiveness; as shared, defensiveness is human AND not conducive in social justice work.

Journal Prompts:

1. Reflect on a microaggression that you have said in the past. Where did that statement/belief originate from? Where did you first hear it?

    _____

    _____

    _____

    _____

2. Thinking about the same microaggression as above, what could you say differently in the future?

    _____

    _____

    _____

    _____

3. Have you ever been the target of a microaggression? How did it make you feel? Do you believe the other person knew the impact of what was said?

    _____

    _____

    _____

    _____

4. Are there some microaggressions in society that you view as 'less offensive'? Why/Why not?

_____

_____

_____

_____

5. Much of this chapter discusses when intentions are positive, but there is still harm. Is it possible for someone's intentions to be negative, but the impact is positive? Why/Why not?

_____

_____

_____

_____

6. Which microaggression (microassault; microinsult; microinvalidation) do you believe is most common? Why do you think that is?

_____

_____

_____

_____

7. Consider watching for stereotypes that are perpetuated in media (social media, news outlets, etc.). How do these stereotypes further divide intentions versus impact?

_____

_____

_____

_____

What does this statement mean to you?

'We must intentionally include so as not to unintentionally exclude.

_____
_____
_____
_____
_____
_____
_____
_____
_____
_____
_____
_____
_____
_____
_____
_____
_____
_____
_____
_____
_____
_____
_____
_____
_____
_____

Many of us have heard of 'open-door policies' – maybe we even tout that we have one in our company. While such policies are a step in the right direction, they are only effective when individuals believe that they will be genuinely listened to and that their contributions are valued. Within the idea of Core Principle #3, we must intentionally include everyone, so no one is unintentionally excluded. Acknowledging that our intentions of having an open-door policy is to encourage communication, it is important to analyze who is actually communicating. The main premise behind this Core Principle is to be proactive when promoting a diverse and inclusive community (whether that be within an organization, a community, a company, a school, and/or a family).

Psychological safety is a critical factor in creating an environment where individuals feel comfortable speaking up and participating fully. It is the belief that one will not face negative consequences or judgment for expressing their thoughts, ideas, and/or concerns. Without psychological safety, even the most well-intentioned open-door policies can fall short. Individuals may hesitate to engage because they fear retribution, ridicule, or being dismissed. For example, in a classroom setting, a student may have a different perspective on a topic being discussed. If they sense that their perspective will be met with criticism or mockery, they may choose to remain silent, limiting the diversity of thought in the class. In addition to providing an environment where different perspectives are welcomed, it is also important to invite and **encourage** different thoughts/perspectives. We grow as a community, organization, and society with the inclusion of different viewpoints.

To foster intentional inclusion, it is essential to build trust within organizations and communities. Trust is the foundation upon which psychological safety is built. This trust includes leaders and peers that will genuinely listen, consider diverse perspectives, and act upon valid concerns. When we embrace the principle of intentional inclusion, we acknowledge that the onus is on us to actively seek out diverse perspectives and voices. We recognize that diversity is not merely about representation, but also about meaningful engagement and inclusion.

There are many benefits of intentional inclusion and diversity of thought amongst a group. First, creativity and innovation are enhanced within a diverse group of people. When individuals from different backgrounds contribute their ideas and experiences, it can lead to more robust and creative solutions. Second, inclusive decision-making processes result in more well-rounded and informed choices. Diverse viewpoints help identify potential blind-spots and consider a broader range of consequences. Third, inclusive communities are more resilient and cohesive.

When individuals feel valued and included, they are more likely to contribute positively to the group's goals and well-being. Lastly, intentional inclusion is a fundamental component of social justice work. It is a means of addressing systemic biases and ensuring that marginalized groups have an equal voice and access to opportunities.

Within social justice transformation, it is crucial to recognize that the burden of ensuring inclusivity cannot fall solely on those who may feel excluded. Rather, it is a collective responsibility that each one of us must actively uphold. While it is essential to create spaces where individuals can voice their concerns, it is equally important not to rely solely on this reactive approach. In many instances, individuals who feel excluded may hesitate to speak up due to fear, discomfort, and/or a sense of powerlessness. They may worry that their concerns will be dismissed or met with resistance. This reluctance to speak up can perpetuate feelings of exclusion and isolation. To provide examples for this, let's look at both a workplace example and a social example. In a workplace, an employee may feel excluded from important decisions and discussions. However, they may not feel comfortable expressing their concerns to their superiors, fearing potential repercussions or alienation. In a social group, a member might experience exclusionary behavior, but choose to remain silent out of fear of confrontation or the desire to avoid making waves. Both of these examples can be addressed by seeking out everyone within a group/organization for their input and to check in. For example, I have often found myself 'on the outside looking in' within social circles. At the same time, once someone invites me to be a part of the conversation and/or activities, I feel seen and tend to interact more with the group. In society, we have heard phrases such as 'Don't just invite me to the dance, ask me to dance.' At US[2], we believe that we must go one step further... Some people don't want to dance. You might think you are being inclusive by asking someone to dance, but they might feel the exact opposite. Instead, when focusing on intentional inclusion, ask people to help you with planning the event that involves them. For example, instead of holding an annual dance, consider bringing together people within the organization/group you are planning for and asking them what they would like to see for the annual gathering. You might be surprised at how amazing the ideas are!

Intentional inclusion places a significant responsibility on those who hold positions of privilege/power and/or belong to the majority group. It calls upon individuals to actively seek out and invite participation from marginalized and/or underrepresented members. It involves recognizing the existence of systemic barriers that hinder inclusion and actively working to dismantle them. We will speak to this idea in much more detail in Section 4.

To expound upon the idea of psychological safety, it's important to understand the elements that contribute to its creation. Being a good listener is foundational to psychological safety. It involves giving others your full attention, asking open-ended questions, and showing empathy. People are more likely to share openly when they know their ideas and perspectives will not be met with judgment. Encourage an atmosphere where diverse viewpoints are welcomed and valued. Consider framing constructive feedback as an opportunity for growth rather than criticism. When individuals feel that feedback is aimed at helping them improve, they are more likely to engage in open dialogue.

Ultimately, we must remember that inclusion is not a passive endeavor, but an active and ongoing commitment. There are quite a few activities that you can consider when looking to intentionally include people within your community, organization, and/or family:

> Seek out those who are quieter in group settings and ask for their feedback. When doing this, it often helps to provide an invitation and context so the person can prepare before the conversation.
> Consider hosting interviews/1:1 conversations on a regular basis to hear from everyone (and not just

those who seek you out). This can be done on a rotating basis or become a shared responsibility if you have a larger team.

> Encourage new ideas by having a portion of agendas dedicated to 'brainstorming'. During this time, no 'blocks' are allowed – simply new ideas for consideration. Encourage everyone to share at least one new idea (giving advance notice for preparation, if needed).

> Ask people within your community/team/class how they can best contribute to a conversation. For example, do they like providing written feedback after a conversation? Maybe they prefer a brief 1:1 conversation before the group discussion to start thinking about the discussion in advance?

Journal Prompts:

1. What do you see as the difference between an 'open-door policy' and intentional inclusion?

   _____

   _____

   _____

   _____

2. Reflect on a time when you felt included and valued in a group or organization. What factors contributed to that sense of inclusion?

   _____

   _____

   _____

   _____

3. Consider an instance where you felt excluded or unheard. How did it affect your participation and engagement? What could have been done differently to make you feel more included?

   _____

   _____

   _____

   _____

4. How would you rank your personal ability to intentionally include others within your community/organization?

_____

_____

_____

_____

5. How does power/privilege play into psychological safety?

_____

_____

_____

_____

6. How can you personally contribute to creating a psychologically safe environment where everyone's voice is valued and heard?

_____

_____

_____

_____

7. Reflecting on this chapter, have you unintentionally excluded anyone, or any group, from a conversation and/or decision? If so, how can you go back and repair that to be able to intentionally include?

_____

_____

_____

_____

What does
this statement mean
to you?

Seek to impact someone's
heart, which will ultimately
change their mind.

_____
_____
_____
_____
_____
_____
_____
_____
_____
_____
_____
_____
_____
_____
_____
_____
_____
_____
_____
_____
_____
_____
_____
_____
_____

One of the many things we say within US[2] is that there are three stages to action: a person must resonate with the material (meaning it must impact their heart) before they remember, and they must remember (meaning it is in their mind) before they can react using the information to change their behaviors. This leads us to our next Core Principle, which focuses on the utmost importance of emotions, vulnerability, and empathy in inspiring meaningful change within society.

In a world driven by data, logic, and facts, it's easy to underestimate the significance of emotions in shaping our beliefs and actions. However, the truth is that even the most analytical individuals ultimately make decisions based on how they feel. Emotions are a force that can drive societal change, and we must recognize their immense power.

In a society where strength and stoicism are often valued, vulnerability is sometimes perceived as a weakness. However, vulnerability is not weakness; it is the courage to expose our true selves. It is in vulnerability that we find our shared humanity. I was often told that showing emotion was a sign of weakness – both in my childhood and as an adult in some of my earlier positions. I learned, however, that my emotions are what made me more relatable and more human. All of us have emotions, and they range from sadness to happiness to anger and many more labels between that. By showcasing our own emotions and allowing them to be shared with the world, we humanize the concept for everyone to be authentically themselves.

Vulnerability and authenticity are powerful tools for creating emotional connections within society. When we allow ourselves to be vulnerable and share our authentic experiences and emotions, we invite others to do the same. This reciprocity builds trust and deepens relationships, leading to societal cohesion. Empathy, the ability to understand and share the feelings of another, is a key element in impacting hearts to change minds. In the realm of social justice, sharing our personal stories of being affected by inequities can evoke empathy and solidarity among those working towards systemic change.

Research in psychology and neuroscience has shown that our brains are wired to prioritize emotionally charged information. When we experience strong emotions in response to something, it creates a memory trace that impacts our behavior more profoundly than raw facts and statistics. Consider the times you've been deeply moved by a story, a film, or a personal experience. Those emotional moments tend to stay with us, often becoming reference points that influence our decisions and actions. To put this into practice, consider something that you remember from being in school. As you reflect on something you remember, there is probably a story attached to it. For example, you might remember a specific assignment that spoke to you. Or maybe you remember a specific teacher because of how they made you feel. Now, did you also learn material in the class? Absolutely! But the material is more easily recovered when you remember it and you are more apt to remember something when it resonates with you emotionally. This can also be seen in marketing. Think about some of the commercials or ads that you remember. Did they make you laugh? Cry? Become nostalgic? The answer to these questions is probably yes (to at least one) and research shows that advertisements that evoke a feeling are more likely to be remembered and influence consumer choices.

In the pursuit of true social transformation, it is essential to recognize that facts alone are insufficient to create meaningful change. While data and statistics provide a rational foundation for change, it is the emotional connection, vulnerability, and empathy that ultimately inspires people to act differently. When we impact someone's heart, we set in motion a ripple effect of change. The emotional connection we feel becomes a catalyst for our own actions and decisions. This ripple effect extends to our interactions with others, creating a chain reaction of positive change. An example of this is a community leader that shares a personal story of resilience, which motivates other community members to support one another and uplift each other through their own struggles. While emotions create a powerful foundation for change, it is essential to channel these feelings into constructive action. We will discuss these action steps further in Section 4.

Ultimately, we must center on humanity and the emotions that connect all of us – and ultimately drive us to action. This is why we believe strongly in sharing personal stories and information that can resonate with an individual. We know that it is only when you are able to resonate with something that you remember it and you are only able to act upon what you remember.

There are quite a few activities that you can consider when looking to impact someone's heart:

> Consider sharing your personal story without trying to persuade someone else to believe something different than their initial thoughts.
> Invite people to share their personal stories about who they are and how they see the world.
> Show gratitude and appreciation for people who listen to your story as well as for those who share their own personal story.
> Ask for permission before sharing your story – remember that our goal is not to change anyone's mind; simply to impact their heart.

Journal Prompts:

1. What types of conversations tend to resonate with you most?

    _____

    _____

    _____

    _____

2. Do you find yourself more focused on statistics or personal anecdotes? Where does that stem from (Were you taught how to communicate in that way)? What value do you see in both modes of communication?

    _____

    _____

    _____

    _____

3. Do you find any particular relationships more difficult to be vulnerable in (i.e., supervisor, colleague, family, community member)? Why do you think that is?

    _____

    _____

    _____

    _____

4. What have you been told throughout your life about emotions? Were you encouraged/discouraged to show emotion as a child? Does your workplace embrace/ encourage emotion?

    _____

    _____

    _____

    _____

5. Has your opinion/viewpoint regarding emotion and vulnerability shifted over the years? If so, how? Why do you think that is?

    _____

    _____

    _____

    _____

6. Have you ever changed your mind about a social issue after hearing more information? What type of information did you hear and how did it impact your opinion?

    _____

    _____

    _____

    _____

7. When interacting with others, how do you view emotion? Do you provide yourself the same grace and compassion that you have for others?

    _____

    _____

    _____

What does this statement mean to you?

'Every issue counts.

_____
_____
_____
_____
_____
_____
_____
_____
_____
_____
_____
_____
_____
_____
_____
_____
_____
_____
_____
_____
_____
_____
_____
_____
_____
_____
_____

In the pursuit of social transformation, it is essential to acknowledge that every person's experiences are valid and worthy of consideration. No single identity is more or less important than another; however, as we will discuss in this chapter, there are some identities that need more attention at any given time because of the immediate danger. It is important to note that having an identity in immediate danger and focusing there does not minimize or invalidate the danger and/or marginalization of other identities.

One of the phrases that is often used within social justice work is the idea of the 'oppression Olympics'. This, in and of itself, is a microaggression. This idea is a harmful mindset where individuals or groups compare their experiences of discrimination, prejudice, or hardship to determine who has suffered the most. This competitive framework can lead to a harmful hierarchy of suffering, where some experiences are deemed more legitimate or deserving of attention than others. In the context of gender discrimination, comparing the experiences of women and non-binary individuals can lead to unproductive debates about who faces more significant challenges, rather than addressing the issue of gender inequality, as a whole. In discussions of racial discrimination, arguing over which racial group faces the most discrimination can divert attention from systemic racism itself, undermining collective efforts to combat it.

The Core Principle of 'Every issue counts' is distinctly different from the idea of 'All lives matter'. While the latter can be used to dismiss or diminish the specific challenges faced by marginalized groups, the former acknowledges that each issue deserves attention and action, without minimizing or invalidating any particular struggle. In a world with a myriad of social justice issues, from immigration reform to racial injustice to gender equality to LGBTQIA+ rights, it can be tempting to prioritize one cause over another. However, the premise behind this Core Principle is that it is our responsibility to address the most pressing issue at a given moment without invalidating the experiences of those affected by other issues. For example, in recent years, society has grappled with a series of pressing issues, from the Black Lives Matter movement to Stop Asian Hate – in addition to women's reproductive rights and transgender rights. While each of these issues is distinct and important, society called upon us to respond to what was most urgent at any given point – without diminishing the other causes and/or struggles.

Embracing the idea that every issue counts encourages a holistic approach to social justice. It allows us to address specific challenges while recognizing the interconnectedness of various forms of discrimination and oppression. This interconnected perspective fosters solidarity among diverse communities and promotes a more comprehensive and inclusive vision of justice.

When we embrace the concept of 'Every issue counts', we foster unity in diversity by encouraging individuals and communities to stand together to transform society. Whether the community is advocating for racial justice, gender equality, or immigrant rights, they recognize that these issues are interconnected (we will discuss the idea of intersectionality deeper later in the book), and their collective efforts create a more powerful force for change.

Every person has a unique story and set of experiences that shape their perspective. Through this Core Principle, in addition to the previous Core Principle discussing the impact of stories, we are invited to respect and honor these individual narratives while encouraging us to create spaces where people can share their stories without fear of judgment or dismissal.

There are quite a few activities that you can consider when looking to validate every experience while also focusing on the identity in most need, at any given moment:

> Identify the identities that are receiving attention in media and consider the different perspectives of people from differing identities.

> Consider listening without a response when someone shares their personal story.
> Make a conscious decision to validate multiple perspectives within a conversation and acknowledge that everyone's perspective is different – based on their own experiences before the conversation.

Journal Prompts:

1. Reflect on a time when you felt that your experiences
    or concerns were invalidated or minimized. How did it
    make you feel, and how did it affect your willingness to
    engage in discussions or actions related to those issues?

    _____

    _____

    _____

    _____

2. Consider a situation where you witnessed someone else's
    experiences being dismissed or downplayed. How did
    you respond, and what strategies can you employ in the
    future to ensure that every issue is treated with respect
    and empathy?

    _____

    _____

    _____

    _____

3. Do you consider some identities 'more impactful' within
    a person's experience in society? Why? Where do those
    beliefs originate from?

    _____

    _____

    _____

    _____

4. Have you ever personally downplayed your own experiences/struggles because you felt they were less 'critical' from other issues/struggles that people may experience? If so, why? Have you ever shared this with anyone? If so, what was their response?

---

5. What is your stance on the controversy between the two statements, "Black lives matter" and "All lives matter"? Why do you think that controversy exists?

---

6. Throughout society, many identities have been targeted (and some have been targeted many times over history). Why do you think that is and how do you believe we can stop the repetitive cycle of oppression?

---

7. What do you believe contributes to the perpetuation of the 'oppression Olympics'? What are you willing to do to embrace everyone's unique stories without minimization?

What does
this statement mean
to you?

Growth occurs in
discomfort.

_____
_____
_____
_____
_____
_____
_____
_____
_____
_____
_____
_____
_____
_____
_____
_____
_____
_____
_____
_____
_____
_____
_____
_____
_____

'Facing new challenges can be uncomfortable – and rewarding. When speaking to social justice work, the transformation that we go through as a society is akin to a workout for the soul, tearing down barriers to make room for growth, and how society can act as a supportive framework to build each other up. To understand the Core Principle of "Growth occurs in discomfort", let's draw an analogy to the physical realm. When you go to the gym, you subject your muscles to discomfort and resistance. The physiology of what is happening is the literal tearing and breaking down of muscle fibers. This stress on muscle fibers is essential because it is only after this breakdown that the muscles rebuild, stronger than before. Muscles rebuild stronger through the introduction of proteins and amino acids to repair the torn muscle fibers. Similarly, in life, discomfort can be seen as the resistance that challenges us. It pushes us to confront our limits, question our beliefs, and adapt to new perspectives. Just as muscles grow stronger through resistance and repair, our minds and characters develop through the discomfort of life's challenges. For example, a person who confronts their fear of public speaking by giving a speech, despite feeling anxious, gradually becomes more confident and skilled in public speaking. In closer alignment with this work, when individuals engage in conversations about sensitive topics like racism, it can be uncomfortable – and it also provides an opportunity to learn, empathize, and challenge existing biases. Through conversations, we become more versed in how to have them, and it becomes less uncomfortable through application and practice.

It is important to discern between being unsafe and being uncomfortable. While discomfort is a natural part of growth, unsafe environments or situations are detrimental and can cause harm. We encourage leaning into discomfort because it often signifies that you are on the brink of something great. In contrast, unsafe spaces are not encouraged and need to be addressed to provide a safe environment. Let's provide an example. When I first started my work in the social justice realm, I was uncomfortable. As a white-presenting woman raised in a very homogenous environment with minimal exposure to diversity, I needed to lean into conversations and be curious A LOT. I found myself asking questions that some may have identified as 'silly' or unnecessary. I made mistakes. However, it was through these mistakes that I learned. It was through asking the tough questions and listening to the responses – even when they weren't pleasant, that I grew.

Healthy discomfort occurs when we step out of our comfort zones, take calculated risks, and face challenges that promote personal and collective growth. It can involve confronting biases, engaging in difficult conversations, or trying new experiences. For example, if a team at work chooses to have a candid discussion about improving collaboration, this may include addressing uncomfortable topics such as power dynamics and communication issues. This healthy discomfort can lead to a more cohesive and effective team.

On the other hand, unsafe environments are those where individuals are at risk of physical, emotional, or psychological harm. These environments cannot be tolerated, and efforts need to be made to address and rectify the issues that make them unsafe. An example of an unsafe environment is a workplace where employees experience harassment or discrimination. It is essential to address such issues promptly through proper channels to ensure the safety and well-being of all employees.

Society plays a pivotal role in shaping our experiences of discomfort and growth. It can serve as a supportive framework, akin to proteins and amino acids, that help rebuild and strengthen individuals after they've faced challenges and discomfort. This support can come in various forms, such as access to education, mental health services, mentorship, or spaces for dialogue.

It is critical to acknowledge that discomfort is not an obstacle, rather an opportunity for personal and collective development. When society acknowledges that discomfort is part of the transformational process of social justice reform, it fosters a culture of resilience. This culture encourages individuals to persevere, learn from experiences, and support one another through challenges. For example, a community that openly discusses mental health and encourages seeking help when needed reduces the stigma surrounding mental health issues. This openness leads to better mental health outcomes and support for those facing difficulties.

Society's role is not only to provide resources, but also to cultivate empathy and compassion. Understanding that everyone faces their unique challenges, society can create spaces where individuals feel heard, valued, and supported. For example, when a society recognizes and empathizes with the challenges faced by marginalized communities, it becomes more inclusive and committed to addressing systemic inequalities. This is also true when companies and/or organizations choose to share a statement regarding current events. It is important to consistently speak up about injustices and allow everyone within the organization, and beyond, to see the organization's commitment to justice.

There are quite a few activities that you can consider when looking to grow through your discomfort:

> Identify your personal 'signs' for being uncomfortable, i.e., increased heart rate, sweaty palms, flushed face.

> Distinguish between being uncomfortable and being unsafe and have those conversations within your community and/or organization.
> Explore ways to build others up after a difficult interaction.
> Invite questions and conversations that may be difficult – acknowledging that growth occurs in discomfort.

Journal Prompts:

1. What are you most proud of accomplishing, up to this point in your life? Was it easy to accomplish? What did you learn while you were working to accomplish this goal/achievement?

   _____

   _____

   _____

   _____

2. How do you feel about the statement, "We appreciate that which we work hard for"? Do you think this statement also relates to social justice work? Why/Why not?

   _____

   _____

   _____

   _____

3. Reflect on a time when you faced discomfort in your personal or professional life. How did this experience contribute to your growth and development?

   _____

   _____

   _____

   _____

4. Consider an uncomfortable situation where you were
   encouraged to lean into discomfort rather than avoid it.
   What positive outcomes emerged from that experience?

   _____

   _____

   _____

   _____

5. How can you support others when leaning into
   discomfort?

   _____

   _____

   _____

   _____

6. Reflect on the difference between being uncomfortable
   and being unsafe. How can you distinguish between the
   two, and what steps can you take to address an unsafe
   situation effectively?

   _____

   _____

   _____

   _____

7. How can you explicitly focus on continual growth?

   _____

   _____

   _____

   _____

What does this statement mean to you?

Once you know better, do better!

_____
_____
_____
_____
_____
_____
_____
_____
_____
_____
_____
_____
_____
_____
_____
_____
_____
_____
_____
_____
_____
_____
_____
_____

Awareness is a first step. And true transformation requires a commitment to change and growth. We cannot be expected to know everything; however, once we know something, it is our responsibility to act upon that knowledge. Within the final Core Principle, we acknowledge that knowledge is a catalyst for personal and societal growth. It signifies that we cannot be held responsible for things we do not know; however, we also cannot use ignorance as an excuse.

Let's start by diving deeper into the idea of using ignorance as an excuse for not taking action toward social justice reform. Although we cannot be expected to know everything (none of us do), it is critical for us to lean into curiosity and ask questions. If you are working in a community that has diverse groups represented that you aren't necessarily familiar with, do your research. As a society, we research things on a regular basis – whether through a YouTube tutorial or asking Siri or Google a question. If you don't know where to start, just start. Asking a simple question like, "What do I need to know about…" will start the learning process.

Learning is a dynamic process that involves seeking knowledge actively, whether through personal experiences, dialogue with others, or access to resources. It is a shared responsibility to educate ourselves about the experiences, challenges, and perspectives of others. A personal example of learning is through experiences.

For example, in my own experience, I had limited exposure to diversity of any sort until after high school; however, once meeting and interacting with people from diverse backgrounds on a personal level, I started to learn more about different identities. Learning can also happen more explicitly, in the form of professional development and/or trainings. For example, a company may provide diversity and inclusion training to its employees with the goal of empowering employees to challenge biases and work toward a more inclusive workplace.

Learning is the process of gaining awareness – or the first step within the Core Principle of "Once you know better, do better". The next step within the Core Principle is to take action and do something with the knowledge gained. If nothing changes after the learning takes place, there is no reason for learning. Mere awareness without corresponding changes in behavior or attitudes is incomplete learning. Incomplete learning occurs when individuals or society as a whole acquire new information or awareness, but fail to translate it into meaningful action or change. For example, a person learns about the environmental impact of single use plastics, but continues to use them without seeking alternatives or reducing their consumption. This either means that the learning didn't resonate with a powerful enough impact, or the person simply chose not to do anything different with the information gained.

Either way, there is no action to remedy the problem of negative environmental impact. Another example is a community that becomes aware of high levels of food insecurity, but does not take action steps to address the issue. Again, either the message was not impactful enough or there was a conscious decision made to not take action toward addressing this concern. We must be willing to take action on issues if we are to work toward true social justice transformation.

To bridge the gap between awareness and action, it is essential to ask questions, seek solutions, and actively engage with the knowledge acquired. Asking questions is a fundamental aspect of learning and growth. It involves curiosity, humility, and a willingness to admit that we do not have all the answers.

Once we have gathered knowledge, we must actively seek solutions and take action to address the issues or challenges we've become aware of. This can involve personal changes, advocacy, support for relevant causes, or community engagement. One example of taking action includes a community becoming aware of a lack of accessible public transportation and then joining together to advocate for improvements and increased accessibility. Another example is an individual who learns about the importance of supporting local businesses and then takes action by shifting their personal shopping habits to prioritize local products and services.

There are quite a few activities that you can consider when looking to gain awareness and ultimately take action:

> - Identify the groups you know little about. Explore. Ask questions. Listen.
> - Dedicate time on a daily or weekly basis for learning. Prompt yourself to ask one question, read one article, listen to one podcast, or watch one video about something you aren't as familiar with.
> - After learning about an issue and/or problem that exists, ask yourself, "What is one thing I can do right now to remedy the inequity?"
> - Find other people to add to your circle that are willing to be accountability partners with you to ensure action steps are taken on a regular basis.

Journal Prompts:

1. How do you best learn new information?

   _____

   _____

   _____

   _____

2. Reflect on a time when you learned something new that challenged your existing beliefs or perspectives. How did you respond to this newfound knowledge?

   _____

   _____

   _____

   _____

3. Consider an issue or challenge in your community, organization, or society that you recently became aware of. What questions can you ask to better understand the root causes and potential solutions?

   _____

   _____

   _____

   _____

4. What issues are you well versed and passionate about? How could you help others within your organization, community, and/or society understand the issue and take action steps?

    _____

    _____

    _____

    _____

5. Reflect on the difference between passive awareness and active learning. What steps can you take to ensure that your knowledge leads to meaningful action and change?

    _____

    _____

    _____

    _____

6. In addition to ensuring that action leads to results, how do you ensure that the action you take is sustained into the future?

    _____

    _____

    _____

    _____

7. What does the concept of 'doing better' mean to you?

    _____

    _____

    _____

    _____

Components of JEDI (Justice, Equity, Diversity, Inclusion) Work

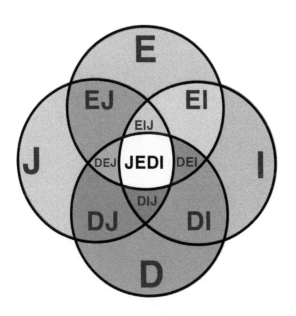

Consider this question

'What is included within social justice transformation?

_____
_____
_____
_____
_____
_____
_____
_____
_____
_____
_____
_____
_____
_____
_____
_____
_____
_____
_____
_____
_____
_____
_____
_____
_____

ow that the foundational principles are established regarding social justice transformation, we must gain common terminology for what is included within JEDI work. Within US², we follow JEDI (Justice, Equity, Diversity, and Inclusion) as our guide for the four components necessary for true transformation. Each of these components is distinct in its meaning and purpose, yet all are connected and necessary within a community for belonging to be present. Please know we use the word community to describe any group of people (whether professional or personal in nature).

Diversity encompasses the rich tapestry of human experiences, backgrounds, and identities. It is a celebration of our differences, recognizing that the world is made vibrant by its variety. Diversity provides a myriad of perspectives and experiences that infuse our society with vitality. By focusing on diversity, we allow one another to be seen in society.

Inclusion is the practice of actively inviting and valuing diverse perspectives and voices. It is about creating spaces where individuals are heard, regardless of their differences. Inclusion is the key that unlocks the power of diversity, allowing it to flourish and contribute to collective growth. Inclusion acts as the bridge between diversity and equity, inviting diverse voices to conversations and decision-making processes, amplifying their impact.

Equity calls for fairness in all aspects of society. It acknowledges that historical and systemic imbalances exist, affecting individuals and communities different-ly. Equity seeks to rectify these imbalances, ensuring that everyone has the opportunity to thrive, regardless of their background or identity, by welcoming them into environments leading to success. Equity ensures that access to opportunities is not prohibitive, espe-cially based upon identities.

Justice is the pursuit of a world where all indi-viduals are valued and treated with dignity. It seeks to dismantle systems of oppression and discrimination, addressing both individual and structural injustices. Justice serves as the North Star, guiding our collective efforts to dismantle oppressive structures, challenge bi-ases, and sustain lasting change.

Throughout this section, we will expand upon each component as well as discuss what happens when any of the four components are missing. Lastly, we will discuss the pinnacle of all four components being present within a community. Everyone deserves to be seen, heard, welcomed, and valued. We have connect-ed these four actions to the four components of JEDI, acknowledging that it is only when all four are strong that there is a sense of respect and belonging. It is my hope that by understanding these four components, you will not only gain knowledge to navigate complex situations, but also be inspired to take action and be-come a catalyst for positive change.

Diversity: Being SEEN

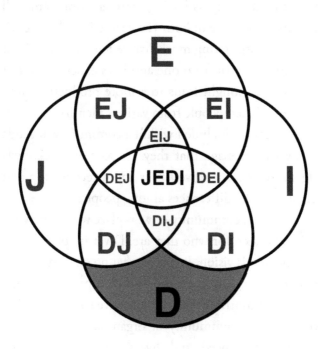

Diversity is more than a buzzword; it is the life-blood of vibrant communities and organizations. According to Merriam-Webster, diversity is the "condition of having or being composed of differing elements, especially the inclusion of people of different races, cultures, etc. in a group or organization". At US², we define diversity as having representation across all identities, inclusive of both visible and invisible identities. By incorporating more diverse representation, not only do you learn from one another's experiences, but diversity of thought leads to a more productive environment. When people from various identities and demographics are included within a community, it sends a powerful message that they are seen and acknowledged. At its heart, diversity is about recognizing and celebrating the differences among people.

Imagine a community or workplace where every individual is seen for who they are. Diversity plays a pivotal role in this vision. It ensures that no one's identity is overlooked or dismissed, and that each person's unique perspective contributes to the collective narrative. Being seen within a community or organization is a fundamental human need, and diversity paves the way for achieving this sense of recognition and visibility.

In the early days, the concept of diversity was primarily rooted in visible identities, or those immediately apparent or perceived by others. It encompassed the recognition of differences such as race, gender, and physical dis/abilities. While this was an important step forward in acknowledging the existence of these distinctions, it was only the start of understanding the diversity amongst us. As our understanding of diversity deepened, we began to recognize that identities extend far beyond the visible. Invisible identities, such as sexuality, religion, socioeconomic background, and mental health, influence our experiences and play a profound role in shaping who we are. Acknowledging these hidden dimensions of identity became an essential aspect of embracing true diversity.

In addition to expanding beyond visible identities, the discussion of diversity has also included many more identities – even including some of them as protected groups. In the early 20th century, the discussion of diversity primarily revolved around gender and/or race; however, as societal awareness grew, the concept of diversity expanded to include a broader range of identities, such as age, sexuality, ability, religion, and cultural background.

In the past, many societies expected individuals from diverse backgrounds to assimilate into the dominant culture. The emphasis was on conformity and uniformity. In contrast, today's understanding of diversity promotes authenticity. It acknowledges and respects different cultural, religious, and social norms, encouraging individuals to express their unique identities without pressure to conform.

Over the last century, many countries have intro-
duced laws and policies to protect the rights of marginalized groups and promote diversity. These legal changes
have been important steps; however, true transformation has also required a cultural shift, where diversity is
embraced not just due to legal obligations, but because
it is seen as a source of strength and innovation.

Initially, diversity was often viewed as a static concept – something defined by fixed categories or char-
acteristics. In recent years, there is growing recognition
that diversity is dynamic and complex. It considers
intersections between various identities, acknowledges
evolving identities and cultures, and understands that
diversity is not a one-size-fits-all concept.

In the past, efforts at diversity sometimes resulted
in tokenism, where a limited number of individuals
from marginalized groups were included simply to
meet quotas. Some of these quotas caused significant
pushback between groups and further polarized our
communities. Today, there is a push for genuine diversity, where diverse perspectives are valued for the
diversity of thought brought to the community.

Diversity initiatives have also evolved from isolated
programs or initiatives into holistic organization-wide
approaches and values. What started as a 'side project'
or isolated 'Diversity Day' in many communities has
evolved to be embedded within the values of communities and organizations. As important as it is to have

an embedded lens of diversity to guide the direction of an organization or community, it is also important to start somewhere. If you find yourself in an environment that hasn't started embracing diversity, an initial project can be a good place to start.

Diversity is critical to embrace for multiple reasons. Diversity fuels innovation. Diverse teams are more likely to generate fresh ideas, challenge the status quo, and find creative solutions to complex problems. In an increasingly competitive global landscape, innovation is a powerful asset. Diverse groups make better decisions. A variety of perspectives ensures a more thorough exploration of potential outcomes, leading to more thoughtful and robust decision-making processes. A diverse community is best served when the institutions that serve it mirror their population. To remain relevant and effective, organizations and communities must ensure they understand, represent, and meet the needs of their constituents. Embracing diversity is also a social responsibility. It is about rectifying historical inequalities, dismantling systemic bias, and advancing social justice. Society's ethical evolution places the onus on institutions and individuals to champion diversity. Finally, in a world connected like never before, having a global perspective is essential. Diversity facilitates cross-cultural competence, helping organizations navigate a complex and interconnected global landscape.

Even with the myriad of benefits shown when implementing and focusing on diversity, some segments of society still struggle with the large-scale implementation and focus on diversity. Most of this struggle originates from a lack of understanding and a fear of the unknown. Fear of the unknown can often lead to a resistance to change – especially when considering the changing of practices or policies because of a diversity initiative. When people are unaware of other identities and/or experiences, biases and stereotypes can be perpetuated. An extreme example of biases and/or stereotypes being perpetuated is cultural appropriation, the borrowing or imitation of elements from one culture by members of another culture.

There are quite a few activities that you can consider when looking to acknowledge diverse identities:

> Educate yourself about the experiences and challenges of others. Read diverse authors, listen to podcasts, and engage with different perspectives.
> Actively seek out relationships with individuals from different backgrounds. Engage in dialogue, build empathy, and broaden your horizons.
> Support initiatives and causes that champion diversity. If you have a platform, whether online or offline, use it to raise up diverse identities. Share stories and perspectives that might not receive mainstream attention.

Journal Prompts:

1. How has your understanding of diversity evolved over time, and what prompted this transformation?

   _____

   _____

   _____

   _____

2. How important is it to you that you are not alone within an organization (i.e., the only woman/person of color)? Why?

   _____

   _____

   _____

   _____

3. Share an experience when you felt truly seen within a community or organization. What made it possible?

   _____

   _____

   _____

   _____

4.   Reflect on the last 10-15 years and the shifts in societal attitudes toward diversity. How have these changes impacted you personally?

_____

_____

_____

5.   What do you see as the primary obstacle(s) to embracing diversity in your workplace or community, and how can they be overcome?

_____

_____

_____

6.   Think about the steps you can take on a personal level to embrace diversity. What small actions can you begin today to make a difference?

_____

_____

_____

7.   Consider listing your identities and put them in two lists: seen and unseen. This does not mean the same as visible and invisible. When referring to seen, what is known and acknowledged within your life (by friends, colleagues, and/or your community)? Unpack what isn't seen and reflect on whether it is because you haven't shared the information or if it is because the identity isn't valued.

_____

_____

_____

Inclusion: Being HEARD

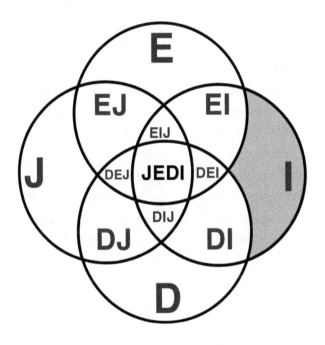

Inclusion is more than an organizational checkbox; it's the heartbeat of thriving communities and organizations. According to Merriam-Webster, inclusion is "the act or practice of including and accommodating people who have historically been excluded (because of their race, gender, sexuality, or ability)". At US², we go one step further with our definition – beyond including people and transitioning to using the information gathered to make informed decisions that include multiple viewpoints. Inclusion entails creating an environment where every individual, regardless of their background, identity, or unique perspectives, not only has a seat at the table, but also a voice in the conversation. Most importantly, true inclusion means that the voice in the conversation impacts decisions that are made.

Imagine a community or workplace where every individual is heard. Beyond simply being listened to, but having decisions made based upon feedback provided. Inclusion plays a pivotal role in this vision. It includes active participation and engagement and ensures that every individual's perspective is integrated into the collective narrative. Inclusion allows people to thrive, knowing that their contributions are heard. Building this sense of inclusion requires proactive efforts, not just passive policies.

Inclusion begins with the simple yet powerful idea that decisions need to be made based on the opinions of diverse voices and, most importantly, hearing from the people that are impacted the most by the decision. At US², we use the phrase, "Nothing about us, without us", which emphasizes the importance of involving individuals most impacted by a decision when shaping policies, practices, and initiatives. This phrase has been true throughout most of our history. The men who founded this country decided that women did not have the right to vote (but they didn't ask for women's opinions); the white men in power decided what people who were enslaved would be 'allowed' to do (without asking for the opinions of the people who were enslaved); hetero-normative lawmakers prohibited same-sex marriage (without asking for the opinions of non-hetero-normative individuals). The list could continue for a very long time. Instead of making decisions FOR others, we need to start including the voices of all people impacted and make decisions WITH others.

Inclusion is not merely a matter of having a diverse group present; it is about validating and valuing the diversity of thoughts and experiences they bring. When inclusion is absent, individuals within an organization may feel ignored and unheard, despite their presence. It's akin to hiring a diverse team but failing to allow their unique perspectives to influence the decisions that are made.

Over the last 50 years, the concept of inclusion has undergone a significant transformation. Initially, inclusion efforts focused on physical accessibility and representation. However, the last 10-15 years have seen a dramatic shift. What was once seen as mere accommodation has become a comprehensive philosophy. Social and political movements have driven conversation on inclusion into the mainstream, emphasizing the need for not just physical accessibility but full participation and representation.

Inclusion is critical to embrace for multiple reasons. Inclusive workplaces boast higher levels of employee engagement, fostering innovation and boosting productivity. Inclusion leads to more well-rounded decision-making and problem-solving. A diverse array of perspectives challenges the status quo and paves the way for more thoughtful, innovative solutions. Inclusive organizations draw top talent from diverse backgrounds, enhancing their adaptability and broadening their reach. Inclusion ensures organizations remain relevant and responsive to an ever-changing, diverse customer base, leading to a more resilient workforce. When people are included in conversations and decisions, there is a feeling of loyalty and appreciation. Without including people's viewpoints in the conversation, ideas will eventually stop flowing – leading to a stagnant environment.

While the concept of inclusion is clear, its consistent implementation can be challenging. Barriers such as implicit/unconscious biases and power dynamics that can dictate how we hear people can hinder progress. As discussed in section 1, implicit/unconscious biases are human and natural. It is essential to recognize any personal biases and work to ensure they don't impact how we hear people. In addition to biases, hierarchies and power imbalances can silence voices and stifle inclusion. Creating a culture of inclusion requires dismantling these barriers and ensuring that all voices are heard, regardless of rank or status within an organization and/or community.

By recognizing the evolution of inclusion, understanding its significance, and addressing its obstacles, we move toward a world where inclusion is the rule, not the exception. In embracing inclusion, we create a world where every individual's unique perspective is celebrated, their contributions matter, and the overarching narrative is truly reflective of humanity.

There are quite a few activities that you can consider when looking to include a variety of voices in your decision-making:

> Give people your full attention when they speak. Listen not just to respond, but to understand.
> Personally invite new voices to conversations and encourage the opposing perspective be shared when making decisions.
> Consider all perspectives and gather as much information as possible when creating policies, procedures, and/or guidelines.

Journal Prompts:

1. How do you understand the concept of inclusion, and how has your perception of it evolved over time?

   _____

   _____

   _____

   _____

2. How important is it to you to be included in conversations where decisions are being made that impact you?

   _____

   _____

   _____

   _____

3. Reflect on an instance when you felt truly heard within a community or organization. What factors contributed to this experience?

   _____

   _____

   _____

   _____

4. Consider the evolution of inclusion over the last 10-15 years. How have societal changes influenced your understanding of inclusion?

_____

_____

_____

_____

5. What are the primary obstacles to inclusion within your workplace or community, and what strategies can address these challenges?

_____

_____

_____

_____

6. Share an instance where your first impression of someone shifted after you listened to their story. How did your perception of that person shift by including their perspective?

_____

_____

_____

_____

7. Reflect on your personal commitment to embracing inclusion. What small actions can you take today to promote inclusion in your community and workplace?

_____

_____

_____

Equity: Being WELCOMED

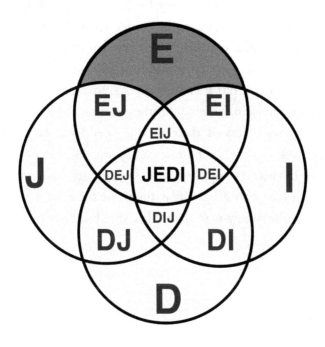

Equity is more than a concept; it's the foundation of a community or organization where every individual is genuinely welcomed and embraced. Equity provides access to opportunities leading to success. It ensures that each person, regardless of their background, identity, or unique attributes, has the same access to opportunity for success. According to Merriam-Webster, equity is "justice according to natural law or right, specifically freedom from bias or favoritism". Equity is often misunderstood as synonymous with equality, but it encompasses a broader and more nuanced vision. Equality implies treating everyone the same, regardless of their unique needs and circumstances. Equity is the practice of ensuring that everyone has access to opportunities and resources necessary to thrive, with a particular focus on those who have been historically marginalized or disadvantaged.

At its core, equity is about providing individuals with the access they need to reach their full potential. It means removing barriers and dismantling obstacles. To illustrate this concept of equality vs. equity and removing barriers, the graphic of three people trying to see a game on the other side of a privacy fence has been widely circulated. In the first image, you see the difference between equality and equity represented visually with each person on the left receiving a box (equality) meaning that the taller person has more than necessary to be able to see while the shorter person still does not have enough height to view over the fence. On the right side of the graphic, the people are given what they need (equity) to be able to see over the fence. This means that the taller person does not need additional support to see over the fence while the shorter person needs two boxes.

EQUALITY   EQUITY

After this graphic was circulated for many years, modifications started to come into circulation. One such modification illustrated a person in a wheelchair (recognizing that the box analogy does not provide access to opportunities for those using mobility devices).

Additionally, another graphic was circulated moving beyond equity. In the image below, the fence is removed completely signifying liberation as the next step after equity.

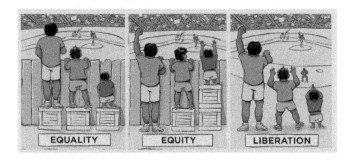

What if I said this graphic still doesn't address everything necessary to promote true access? Rather than simply eliminating the fence, what if we took the time to analyze if there was a reason for it to be there in the first place? The intention behind this graphic is that the fence stands for systemic oppression that exists in society and we must eliminate it to be liberated as a community. At the same time, if we simply remove everything that is seen as an obstacle without asking questions and learning why it was put there in the first place, we are doomed to repeat the same mistakes.

Instead of completely removing the fence, I recommend transitioning into an option that provides access while still keeping society safe. Sticking with this metaphor, what if a ball started coming toward the fence? Without a fence there, there would be no protection. In addition, many venues of today require a single entry point for security measures. Without a fence, there is a stronger possibility of safety breaches. Ultimately, my question to all of you reading this book is: How can we ensure access to opportunities while still learning from the mistakes of our past? We must be reminded of the errors made in our past so that we don't repeat them. The image below covers all of the concerns discussed: access, maintaining safety protocols, and keeping record of our past so we can learn for the future.

Initially, equity efforts primarily focused on addressing overt discrimination. However, the last 10-15 years have seen a dramatic shift in how society perceives and champions for equity. Equity has moved beyond addressing individual acts of discrimination to challenging the very systems and structures that perpetuare inequality.

Equity is critical to embrace for multiple reasons. Equity ensures that all individuals have access to opportunities and resources, regardless of their backgrounds, and is a powerful tool for reducing disparities in opportunities, outcomes, and quality of life. Equitable societies are more cohesive, as they reduce disparities that can lead to divisions and conflict. Equity also fosters economic growth by tapping into the full potential of all individuals, contributing to increased productivity and profitability. And, most importantly, embracing equity is an ethical imperative as it aligns with principles of fairness and human rights.

Despite the undeniable importance of equity, challenges persist. Many people, especially those who have benefited from privilege, may perceive equity efforts as a threat. This resistance often stems from a misunderstanding of equity's goals and consequences. Some individuals view equity as a form of oppression (i.e., reverse racism), assuming that efforts to level the playing field result in the unfair treatment of privileged groups. It is crucial to clarify that equity seeks justice, not revenge. Navigating the resistance to equity can be challenging. It requires effective communication, education, and a commitment to demonstrating the benefits of equity for all. In embracing equity, we create a world where everyone has a chance to reach their full potential, where disparities are replaced by equity, and where fairness and justice are the cornerstones of every community and organization.

Neglecting equity has significant consequences for individuals, organizations, and society as a whole. When equity is not prioritized, disparities persist and injustices endure. Without equity, marginalized groups continue to face systemic barriers that limit their access to opportunities, leading to ongoing cycles of disadvantage. Inequities breed social unrest and discontent – just look at the last 7-10 years if you need any more proof of this. We must be willing to look in the mirror and ask ourselves what we can do to ensure that everyone has access to opportunities for success. Some ways to do this include:

> Reflect on identities that you hold which society affords privilege to (i.e., white, male, Christian, cisgender, heterosexual). Consider ways that you can amplify marginalized voices who don't have the same identities of privilege.

> Speak up when you see access afforded to only certain groups.

> Explore policies within your community and/or organization. Who do these policies (either explicitly or implicitly) restrict access for? Consider bringing attention to these policies and offering solutions to provide access for all.

Journal Prompts:

1. What is your personal understanding of equity, and how has it evolved over time?

   _____

   _____

   _____

   _____

2. Reflect on an instance when you felt genuinely welcomed and supported within a community or organization. What made this experience unique?

   _____

   _____

   _____

   _____

3. How have the perceptions of equity transformed over the last 10-15 years, and what societal changes have driven this shift?

   _____

   _____

   _____

   _____

4. Consider the misconceptions surrounding equity, such as the notion that it leads to oppression. Have you encountered these misconceptions in your personal or professional life? How can they be addressed and dispelled?

_____

_____

_____

5. Consider the primary obstacles to achieving equity within your community or workplace. What strategies can address these challenges?

_____

_____

_____

6. Share a situation where you advocated for equity or challenged inequities. What were the outcomes of this experience?

_____

_____

_____

7. Imagine a world where equity is fully realized. What does that world look like, and how does it differ from the present? What steps can you take to contribute to the realization of this vision?

_____

_____

_____

Justice: Being VALUED

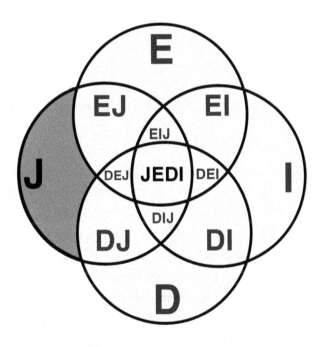

Justice is the foundation of a community where every individual is valued and cherished. It represents the true realization of social transformation. According to Merriam-Webster, social justice is "a state or doctrine of egalitarianism – a social philosophy advocating the removal of inequalities among people". Ultimately, within US², we define justice as the opportunity to value everyone as individuals and address historical and ongoing inequities to ensure a more just society in the future.

Imagine a world where the concept of justice is synonymous with fairness and equality. A world where systemic and systematic biases within society no longer form barriers that hinder individuals from reaching their full potential. To truly achieve social justice reform, we must aspire to eliminate these obstacles. Within justice, we move beyond simply seeing someone (as represented by diversity), hearing someone (as represented by inclusion), and welcoming someone (as represented by equity). Within justice, we work explicitly to value the uniqueness of every individual. Justice is the guardian of human worth and the key to valuing every individual within a community or organization.

In the past, justice spoke specifically to the legal system and criminal matters. It now encompasses social justice, economic justice, and environmental justice. This modern definition recognizes that societal disparities are interconnected and require comprehensive solutions.

Justice is not a passive concept. It demands action – action that is informed, deliberate, and comprehensive. Without action, the aspirations of this work remain unfulfilled. Action that is informed requires careful planning and systemic reform. Deliberate action is tied to tangible actions and achieves measurable results. Last, but not least, justice must move beyond talking the talk. It must also move beyond walking the walk – if desired results are not being met. At US², we equate this to getting off the treadmill of social justice work. If you are staying busy 'doing' things, but not seeing the desired results, it is your responsibility to adjust and take different action steps.

Justice, when embodied through action, becomes a force for transformation. It is the process of rectifying historical wrongs, dismantling oppressive systems, and ensuring that every individual is valued and empowered. Justice requires acknowledging and addressing historical injustices that continue to reverberate through generations. It means confronting the legacies of discrimination, colonization, and oppression. Justice involves taking systematic actions to dismantle deeply ingrained biases within institutions and systems. It means reevaluating policies, practices, and structures to ensure they promote fairness and equality. Justice calls for accountability. It requires holding individuals, organizations, and institutions responsible for their actions and decisions. This accountability ensures that justice is not merely an ideal, but a reality. Lastly, true justice empowers marginalized communities by creating opportunities for economic, social, and political advancement.

Justice, and the interpretation of justice, is often wrought with conflict. The complexities and limitations of legal systems can sometimes hinder justice. In addition, disparities in access to resources and opportunities can undermine justice initiatives. Most prevalent, though, in the obstruction of justice reform is the influence of politics. While political parties were originally created to provide a voice to the people, it has been reinforced for centuries, especially in the US, that politicians often provide a voice to the people they align with. Until we can have open, honest conversations with all perspectives represented, it will be difficult to align justice within the political system.

There are quite a few activities that you can consider when looking to value everyone's unique attributes within a community:

> Encourage open and respectful dialogue about social justice issues within your community.
> Actively participate in social justice initiatives, challenging status quo and reforming policies.

> Before entering into a discussion with some-
one, identify at least one valuable trait about
them. If you can't identify something valuable
within them, justice will not result from the
conversation.

Journal Prompts:

1. Reflect on your personal understanding of justice and its significance in valuing individuals within a community or organization.

_____

_____

_____

_____

2. Share an instance when you observed a just decision or act within your community or workplace. What made this experience significant?

_____

_____

_____

_____

3. Consider the distinction between talking about justice and taking meaningful action. Can you think of instances where organizations or individuals talked the talk but failed to walk the walk? How can we bridge the gap between words and actions?

_____

_____

_____

_____

4. How has the concept of justice evolved over the last 10-15 years? What societal changes have driven this evolution?

_____

_____

_____

_____

5. Consider the primary obstacles to achieving justice within your community or workplace. What strategies can address these challenges?

_____

_____

_____

_____

6. Imagine a world where justice is fully realized. What changes do you envision in your community or society? How can you contribute to the realization of this vision through your actions?

_____

_____

_____

_____

7. Reflect on your role in promoting justice, both as an individual and as a member of your community or organization. What concrete steps can you take to advance justice in your sphere of influence?

_____

_____

_____

_____

Consider this question

'What happens when one (or more) of these components are missing?

_____
_____
_____
_____
_____
_____
_____
_____
_____
_____
_____
_____
_____
_____
_____
_____
_____
_____
_____
_____
_____
_____
_____
_____
_____

Social justice reform is multifaceted, comprised of diversity, inclusion, equity, and justice. Neglecting any of these components results in an incomplete puzzle. Within this section, we will discuss the trajectory of what happens when organizations focus on select components of the JEDI framework, rather than all four components.

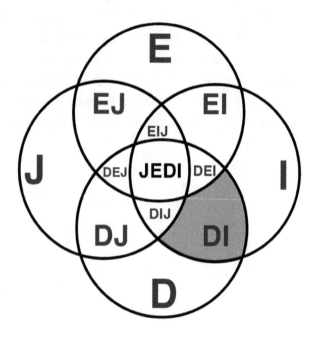

When society started to focus on issues surrounding social justice, equity, diversity, and inclusion, many organizations gravitated toward D&I work (focusing specifically on diversity and inclusion). However, focusing solely on these two facets will often lead to a strictly quantitative approach that emphasizes numbers over systemic change. Remember, when breaking these down, you are focusing on SEEing and HEARing your constituents. Without welcoming and/or valuing what is seen and/or heard, organizations may prioritize numerical targets over the lived experiences and well-being of individuals.

Imagine an organization that places a strong emphasis on increasing its diversity numbers, setting ambiguous targets for hiring individuals from various backgrounds. These efforts may lead to a more diverse workplace with representation from marginalized groups; however, if the organization neglects to address systemic biases, inequities in promotions, or microaggressions, it risks reducing diversity efforts to a mere numbers game.

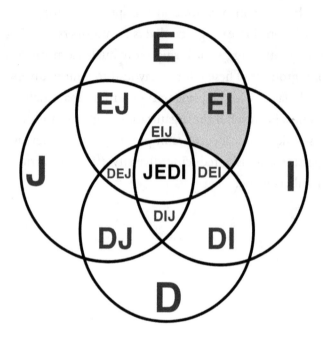

In addition to companies focusing on diversity and inclusion, some organizations chose to focus on equity and inclusion. Combining equity and inclusion without the other components can inadvertently reinforce a phenomenon known as the 'savior complex'. Equity seeks to WELCOME constituents while inclusion seeks to HEAR constituents. Without the focus on diversity, there is a lack of representation and without the incorporation of justice, there is a lack of actionable steps being taken. Oftentimes, organizations that follow the EI model are often stuck in sympathy, rather than empathy.

Imagine an organization that places a strong emphasis on equity and inclusion, with privileged individuals taking on leadership roles in diversity and inclusion initiatives. These leaders may be genuinely committed to creating a fair and inclusive environment; however, the approach can inadvertently create a dynamic where those with privilege are seen as the saviors or heroes of marginalized individuals. In this scenario, the agency and voices of marginalized individuals may be sidelined, with well-intentioned individuals assuming the role of rescuers. This savior complex can perpetuate imbalances of power and hinder the true empowerment of marginalized groups.

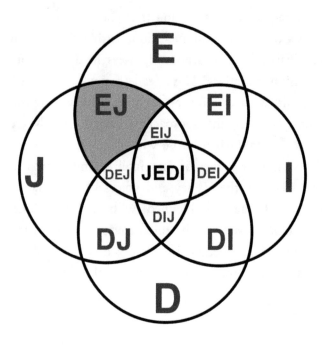

When the focus is solely on justice and equity, a critical element may be overlooked: the need for clear metrics and benchmarks to measure progress. Justice is about rectifying historical wrongs and dismantling oppressive systems by VALUING individuals, while equity seeks to level the playing field by providing access and WELCOMING individuals. Without robust metrics (that are often found within diversity and inclusion efforts), it becomes challenging to gauge the effectiveness of these efforts.

Imagine embarking on a journey without a map or a compass. You may have the best of intentions, but without clear guidance, you risk meandering aimlessly. This lack of direction may result in getting to your destination, but solely by luck and coincidence. Without a map, there is no way to repeat the same results – meaning there is a significant drop in sustainability. In the realm of social justice reform, this translates to well-intentioned initiatives that lack the necessary direction to create lasting change. The absence of measurable outcomes can leave both leaders and constituents uncertain about the true impact of their actions.

Measuring progress is not about reducing complex social issues to mere numbers; it's about ensuring that efforts are effective and that intended outcomes are achieved. Metrics provide a sense of direction, helping organizations and individuals navigate the often intricate path of social justice reform. Without them, well-intentioned actions may fall short of creating the transformative change we aspire to see.

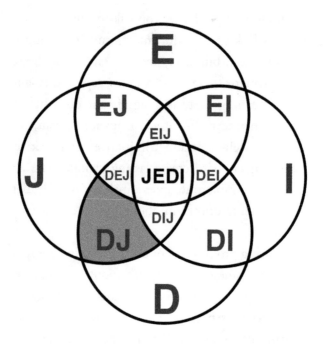

When justice and diversity are the sole focus, a common pitfall is the presence of diversity without the corresponding impact on decisions and outcomes. Diversity celebrates the representation of individuals from various backgrounds (SEEing people), while justice aims to address historical injustices and VALUE people. However, the mere presence of diverse individuals does not guarantee meaningful change.

Imagine assembling a diverse team of individuals from different backgrounds. Their perspectives, experiences, and backgrounds offer a wealth of potential insights and solutions. However, if organizational decisions and processes remain unchanged, the diverse perspectives may remain untapped. The result is a missed opportunity for innovation and a failure to harness the full potential of representation. In this scenario, decisions continue to be made without considering the diverse perspectives at the table (what you would find within inclusion). The consequences of such decisions may perpetuate systemic biases and inequities, ultimately hindering progress.

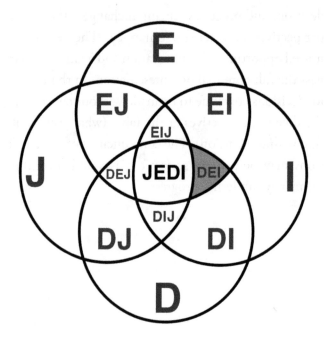

Very commonly used today is the acronym DEI, standing for a focus on diversity, equity, and inclusion. However, addressing diversity, equity, and inclusion without the guiding light of justice can lead to well-intentioned efforts lacking transformative impact. Diversity acknowledges uniqueness and representation; inclusion ensures that decisions are made after hearing all constituents; equity levels the playing field by providing access to opportunities. However, without justice and a true sense of value for all constituents, these efforts may stay surface-level or appear as checkboxes that are pursued for 'show' rather than meaningful change.

Imagine an organization that prominently features diversity, equity, and inclusion initiatives in its corporate culture. It may invest in diversity training, create inclusive policies, and celebrate accomplishments and achievements of historically marginalized groups; however, if systemic biases and inequities are not addressed at the foundational level, these efforts can become symbolic gestures rather than drivers of true change. In this scenario, individuals may perceive these initiatives as mere checkboxes or superficial efforts to portray a progressive image. The absence of justice means that the root causes of inequity and discrimination persist, undermining the potential for meaningful transformation.

Journal Prompts:

1. Reflect on experiences where you have encountered efforts that focus on only one or two of the four components. What were the strengths and limitations of these efforts?

   _____

   _____

   _____

   _____

2. Reflect on your current work environment. What components are you addressing consistently? What are your constituents told that you address consistently?

   _____

   _____

   _____

   _____

3. Reflect on your personal skillset in relation to all four components. What do you see as your strength? What could you improve upon further?

   _____

   _____

   _____

   _____

4. Consider researching organizations and/or communities
    that have showcased their efforts in one (or more) of the
    components. Do you believe that they are 'walking the walk'
    in addition to simply 'talking the talk'? How do you know?

    _____

    _____

    _____

    _____

5. Reflect on the trajectory of society with relation to the
    four components. What do you feel we have focused on
    during different times in history?

    _____

    _____

    _____

    _____

6. What can you personally do to strengthen the integration
    of missing components within your community?
    Consider brainstorming ideas for all four components.

    _____

    _____

    _____

    _____

7. Do you believe that one of the four components is easier
    to implement? More difficult? Why?

    _____

    _____

    _____

    _____

'What results when all four
components are present?

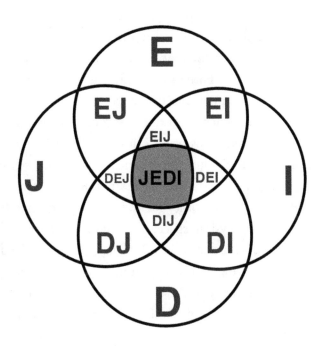

In the realm of social justice reform, the truest transformation occurs when all four components operate in unison – leading a true sense of belonging. This holistic approach creates an environment where individuals not only coexist, but thrive, fostering a profound sense of belonging and respect.

Imagine an organization or community where all four components coalesce seamlessly. Here, diversity is not just about numerical representation, but about the celebration of differences. Equity is a guiding principle that ensures fairness for all. Inclusion extends beyond mere acceptance to create a deep sense of being heard. Justice is not an abstract concept, but a tangible force that rectifies historical injustices. In such an environment, individuals experience a profound sense of belonging that transcends the boundaries of race, gender, age, or any other identity. Belonging extends beyond the physical space; it permeates hearts and minds. People are seen, heard, welcomed, and valued for who they are, their backgrounds, and lived experiences. The synergy of these four components fosters a sense of belonging and genuine respect that transcends differences.

In a space where all four components thrive, respect takes on a profound meaning. It moves beyond mere tolerance or coexistence and becomes a cornerstone of interactions. Individuals not only acknowledge each other's differences, but deeply respect them. Respect, in this context, is an active practice of recognizing the inherent worth and dignity of every person.

Let's imagine another scenario... Imagine a workplace or community where respect is not just a policy, but a way of life. Diversity is not a check-box, but a source of strength and innovation. Equity is not about providing the same things to everyone; rather, providing the necessary access for everyone to be successful. Inclusion goes beyond lip service, creating spaces where individuals are heard – and decisions are impacted by their opinions. And justice is not just a concept, but a reality that actively dismantles barriers and values everyone as their authentic selves. In such an environment, respect is not a passive sentiment; it is an active commitment. People actively seek to understand each other's experiences and perspectives. They acknowledge that each person's journey is unique, shaped by their background and identities.

The transformative power of holistic commitment extends beyond individuals to the broader community or organization. When all four components are present and actively embraced, their impact ripples through every aspect of the organization or community. In such an environment, the organization thrives. Creativity and innovation flourish because diverse perspectives lead to out-of-the-box thinking.

Employee morale is high, turnover is low, and the organization attracts top talent. The commitment to justice means that discrimination is actively challenged and rectified, creating access to opportunities for everyone.

Journal Prompts:

1. Reflect on an experience when you felt a profound sense of belonging within a group or organization. What factors contributed to this feeling of belonging?

    _____

    _____

    _____

    _____

2. Consider the role of respect in your personal and professional relationships. How do you actively practice respect in your interactions with others? Is it different between personal and professional relationships?

    _____

    _____

    _____

    _____

3. What do you see as the biggest obstacle for companies/organizations trying to implement the holistic approach of JEDI? Why is that an obstacle?

    _____

    _____

    _____

    _____

4. Who do you believe is a company and/or person that embodies all four components? Why do you feel this way? How do they showcase their commitment?

    _____

    _____

    _____

    _____

5. Do you believe there are any elements missing from the JEDI model? If so, what are they?

    _____

    _____

    _____

    _____

6. Reflect on your role in promoting a holistic approach to social justice reform. How can you actively contribute to creating spaces where all four components thrive?

    _____

    _____

    _____

    _____

7. What can you do immediately to equip yourself with information to increase your ability to embrace all four components of JEDI work?

    _____

    _____

    _____

    _____

SECTION THREE

Stages of Metamorphustice™

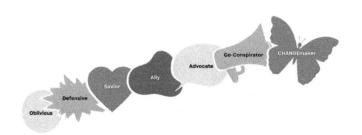

Consider this question

'Why is social justice reform called metamorphustice™?

In a world brimming with diversity and complexity, where individuals from various backgrounds and experiences coexist, and polarization has become the primary 'go-to', the pursuit of social justice has never been more paramount. The issues we face as a global community are vast and intricate, touching upon areas as diverse as racial equity, gender equity, economic fairness, and much more. The urgency of addressing these concerns is evident, as the repercussions of inaction loom large. Within this intricate web of social challenges, the journey of social justice reform is not merely a series of actions and reactions. It is a profound process of transformation that encapsulates the dynamic evolution required in the realm of social justice.

Metamorphustice™, as a concept, is a juxtaposition of 'metamorphosis' and 'justice', signifying the comprehensive transformation necessary to address the intricacies and interconnections of social injustices. It acknowledges that achieving social justice is not a linear or one-dimensional path, but a transformation that involves a series of stages, all leading to profound change. This idea reflects the profound process of societal self-reflection and evolution. It is only through true transformation that we can ensure a more empowering and just society.

Within metamorphustice™, there are seven stages – each stage representing a new attribute or characteristic that progresses someone through the transformational continuum.

In the first stage of Oblivious, there is a lack of awareness and acknowledgement of the issues experienced by marginalized identities. This starting point is one where many individuals find themselves, often due to upbringing, limited exposure, or societal insulation. The initial step in the process of metamorphustice™ is recognizing this lack of awareness and embarking on the path toward greater understanding.

In the second stage of metamorphustice™, Defensive, individuals begin to confront the reality of social injustices. Within this stage, discomfort often arises, leading to a resistance to change. This stage is a pivotal point where acknowledging the need for transformation, through care and concern, can lead to personal growth or perpetuate the status quo. It is important to note that people can become defensive of their own identities as well as other identities. This defensiveness is rooted in a sense of strong emotion.

The third stage of metamorphustice™, Savior, is marked by a well-intentioned, but often misguided, desire to 'rescue' others from oppression. It arises from an unconscious belief in one's superiority and a sense of responsibility to 'save' those seen as less fortunate. In this stage, individuals must recognize their latent biases and transition toward a more genuine allyship rooted in curiosity.

The next stage of metamorphustice™, Ally, is the first step toward change. Allies are characterized by sympathy for others and often serve as a shoulder to cry on, building bridges between different communities. However, having sympathy is not enough for true transformation. Empathy is needed – and the attribute attached to the next stage of the transformational process of metamorphustice™.

Advocates, the fifth stage within metamorphustice™, move beyond sympathy and become active voices for marginalized communities. They utilize their privilege and position to speak up and make a difference on behalf of marginalized identities.

While Advocates speak up on behalf of others, Co-Conspirators, the sixth stage of metamorphustice™, empower others to use their voices. Instead of using their privilege to speak up for others, they use their privilege to provide opportunities for others who may be marginalized so they can speak for themselves.

The final stage within metamorphustice™ is that of CHANGEmaker. This final stage represents true transformation by being proactive and actively seeking out opportunities for change rather than waiting for something to be brought to light. They understand that justice is a constant pursuit, and they are dedicated to being the driving force behind that pursuit.

The stages of metamorphustice™ represent a progression, but they are not linear. People may find themselves moving between stages, facing their biases and weaknesses specific to particular identities, and striving to evolve continually. The process through these stages is marked by self-awareness, education, and a commitment to action.

The pursuit of metamorphustice™ is vital because it redefines social justice as a collective endeavor that begins with the individual. It underscores the importance of self-awareness and self-improvement as the initial steps to achieving meaningful, lasting change within society. It calls upon every individual, irrespective of their background or experiences, to participate actively in the transformation required to address social injustices.

Metamorphustice™ places social justice reform in the context of personal growth and transformation. It highlights the inseparable connection between understanding ourselves and our relationships with others with uniting society. The framework encourages individuals to adopt a proactive approach to justice by challenging their biases, embracing empathy and curiosity, and taking constructive action.

As we journey through this exploration of metamorphustice™, I will delve into each stage, examining the challenges and opportunities they present. Along the way, I will invite you to consider how personal transformation leads to societal change, and journal prompts will be provided to facilitate self-reflection and action. Join this transformative journey, as we explore the stages of metamorphustice™ and work together to build a more just and equitable world.

Stage 1: Oblivious

Oblivious

"'We cannot be expected to understand
something we have not experienced; however,
ignorance cannot be used as an excuse."

'In the vast tapestry of human existence, we each occupy a unique thread – shaped by our upbringing, surroundings, and experiences. Sometimes, our threads intertwine, weaving together stories of shared histories and common understandings. Other times, our threads remain isolated, insulated within a protective bubble of familiarity. It is within this bubble that the first stage of social justice reform, Oblivious, takes form.

I grew up in what I lovingly call the "White Lake Bubble". Growing up, I was surrounded by people that looked like me, being taught about people who looked like me by people who looked like me, with minimal exposure to anyone outside of my bubble due to having very little money (leading to a lack of travel and outside experiences). In addition to the visible similarities, I was also surrounded by lifestyle similarities. Everyone, with the exception of one family, celebrated Christian holidays (the one family that didn't were Jehovah Witness – all I knew was that they had to sit in the office when there were any celebrations). We were never taught about other cultures (aside from some of the stereotypical representations). I say this to also say that I graduated from a great school. Many of my classmates became doctors, lawyers, and very influential within their field. I formed great relationships with many of my teachers – and some of which I still maintain today. AND, I was oblivious to the diversity that surrounds us up until college. I wasn't necessarily 'sheltered' or kept away from diverse identities on purpose, we simply didn't have exposure within the environment I spent my time in. And as I have continued this work, I have heard so many people sharing a similar experience. We know what we are exposed to (whether intentionally or unintentionally). Without explicit exposure and awareness of multiple identity groups, we can find ourselves in the first stage of metamorphustice™, Oblivious.

Obliviousness is a stage characterized by a lack of awareness about experiences, perspectives, and realities beyond our own. It's not about fault or intention – it's about living in a bubble that shields us from the vast diversity of human existence. At this stage, individuals may find themselves surrounded by people who share their background, look like them, and think like them. They may not have had the opportunity to engage with different cultures, identities, or worldviews.

Imagine growing up in a place like I did in White Lake, where the world around you seemed to mirror your own reflection. You attended schools where your teachers resembled you, teaching a curriculum centered on people who looked like you. The community you were a part of predominantly shared your background and experiences. In this environment, there can be a sense of comfort; however, there can also be a sense of insulation and fear of anything (or anyone) different. This bubble of obliviousness is not unique to one place or one person – it exists wherever we find ourselves surrounded by the familiar, where everyone we know looks and thinks like us. It's a natural human tendency to seek out comfort and similarity, and it can inadvertently create blind spots in our understanding of the world.

In the Oblivious stage, individuals may recount experiences that are somewhat insular. They may recall a lack of exposure to diverse perspectives, cultural backgrounds, or identities different from their own. For example, many people who find themselves in the Oblivious stage share growing up or living in communities where everyone shares a similar racial, ethnic, or cultural background. In addition to homogenous surroundings, people within this stage report rarely encountering people from different cultural or religious backgrounds, leading to a limited understanding of their customs and traditions. Lastly, by experiencing an education system, media, or social circles dominated by a single narrative or perspective, diverse voices are excluded. I personally experienced all three of these. I left for college thinking that there was only one way to live in the world and that everyone had similar life experiences as myself. What I didn't realize was how wrong I was – and how damaging that obliviousness was for both myself and those I interacted with.

During the Oblivious stage, others may perceive you as someone who lacks exposure to the richness of human diversity. Your interactions may be characterized by a limited worldview, shaped primarily by your own experiences. People might not fault you for this, but they may sense a certain lack of awareness about the broader spectrum of human existence. Although you are not at fault for initially being in the Oblivious stage, once you are aware of what you don't know, ignorance cannot be used as an excuse.

Remaining in the Oblivious stage can have profound consequences. It may lead to unintentional harm through perpetuating stereotypes, reinforcing biases, and contributing to systemic inequities. It can hinder meaningful connections with people from diverse backgrounds and limit one's ability to contribute to positive change. Without firsthand exposure to diverse groups, individuals may rely on stereotypes and assumptions to fill in the gaps of understanding. Obliviousness can reinforce existing biases, as individuals have not had the chance to challenge or reevaluate their beliefs. Empathy often grows from exposure to the experiences and hardships of others. Obliviousness can hinder the development of empathy. Obliviousness may also result in individuals unintentionally contributing to systemic inequities by not recognizing their existence.

If you find yourself in the Oblivious stage, the most important attribute to build upon when progressing into the next stage of metamorphustice™ is awareness. Actively seek opportunities to interact with individuals from different backgrounds. Attend cultural events, engage in discussions with diverse groups, and read books or watch documentaries that broaden your horizons. Take the initiative to learn about various cultures, histories, and identities. Challenge your own biases and preconceptions.

If you are helping someone else progress from the Oblivious stage, encourage them to explore new experiences and engage with diverse communities. Remember that it is only once we understand ourselves that we can work to understand others and then ultimately unite society. It is important to remember this when supporting others in different stages of their personal transformation. We must do our own work before supporting others in their work.

While obliviousness may not be a deliberate choice, it is a stage where growth and transformation can begin. The key is to recognize the bubble you inhabit and to actively seek opportunities to venture beyond it. The transition from Oblivious to the subsequent stages of social justice reform is marked by a level of awareness – a willingness to learn, explore, and engage with the diverse narratives that make up our world. The Oblivious stage is not a place of blame, but an opportunity to awaken to the broader human experience.

The thread of oblivion can bind us in a cocoon of familiarity. It's a natural inclination to seek comfort with the familiar, surrounded by the reflections of ourselves. However, this comfort can inadvertently lead to a lack of awareness – a state of obliviousness – about the vast diversity of human existence.

The journey of social justice reform begins with the recognition that ignorance, or lack of awareness, cannot serve as an excuse. We cannot be expected to understand something we have not experienced, and we must acknowledge that our lack of understanding is an invitation to learn, not a justification for perpetuating stereotypes, biases, or systemic inequities. To progress from the Oblivious stage, we must become aware – aware of our own limitations, biases, and the diversity of human identities that exist beyond our own. It is through this awareness that we can unravel the threads of our cocoon and venture into the broader world, ready to embrace diverse perspectives and experiences. Awareness is the key that unlocks the door to the subsequent stages of social justice reform. So, let us remember that ignorance, or lack of awareness, may be where we begin, but it is not where we must stay.

The Oblivious stage is a starting point – a place to recognize our limitations and the potential for growth and awareness. As Core Principle #7 states, once we know better, once we become aware, we must take steps to do better. The transformation of social justice is a continuous process of learning, un-learning, and evolving toward a more inclusive and equitable world.

Journal Prompts:

1. Think about where you grew up. Were you surrounded by people/curriculum/events that honored and mirrored you as an individual? How did this shape your understanding of self, and others?

    _____

    _____

    _____

    _____

2. Take a moment to think about your close friends and acquaintances. Do they mostly resemble you in terms of background, identity, and/or beliefs? How might this affect your perspective?

    _____

    _____

    _____

    _____

3. Think about the books you've read, movies you've watched, and the news sources you follow. Are they diverse in terms of cultural representation and perspectives, or do they primarily align with your own?

    _____

    _____

    _____

    _____

4. Think about phrases and/or beliefs you may have heard
    as a child. Are there some of those that you have found
    to be untrue as you expanded your circle of influence?

    _____

    _____

    _____

5. Reflect on your personal sphere of influence (work,
    personal, or community). How do you believe your lack
    of awareness regarding social justice issues impacts the
    people around you?

    _____

    _____

    _____

6. Consider the impact of ignorance/lack of awareness
    and the perpetuation of social injustices. Can you think
    of any real-world examples where ignorance has led to
    discrimination or marginalization?

    _____

    _____

    _____

7. Imagine a future where people progress beyond the
    Oblivious stage. What are some steps that people can
    take to increase awareness of other identities?

    _____

    _____

    _____

Stage 2: Defensive

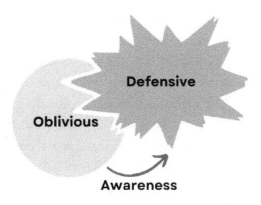

"'You can benefit from an identity of privilege without having lived a privileged life."

The journey through the stages of social justice reform is neither straightforward nor simple. It's a transformative process marked by self-discovery and, inevitably, discomfort. After emerging from the oblivion of our own limited perspectives, we often find ourselves at a crossroads that we call the Defensive stage. This stage is a turbulent landscape where personal awareness collides with profound emotions, some of which we never expected to encounter.

After growing up in a very homogenous environment, I was in for one of the greatest 'shocks' of my life when I was placed in the International dorm for my first year of college. I wasn't going to college with anyone from high school and I definitely wasn't living with anyone I knew. I was going from being an only child with my own room and no siblings to sharing a small space with three other people that I never met before. Upon arriving on campus, I realized very quickly that I wasn't in White Lake anymore. In addition to the campus being fairly diverse (and definitely much more diverse than where I spent the first 17 years of my life), I was living in a building with people from all over the world. Walking down the hallways, I remember hearing languages I had never heard before (let's be honest, the only language I had heard to that point in my life besides English was Spanish which I took four years of in high school and still wasn't fluent). I remember smelling foods I had never smelled before (all being cooked in a dual function 'micro-fridge' – microwave and refrigerator combined). Soon after arriving on campus, I became more involved with different student groups and started my own personal social justice transformation. As I started to learn more about the truth of our history and hearing about the lived experiences of so many of my classmates, I became angry. I was angry for what my ancestors did. I was angry for what my ancestors didn't do. I was sad for what so many people had experienced – and continued to experience on a daily basis. I felt guilt and shame attached to who I was and, most importantly, who I represented in my visible identities. This stage of guilt, shame, and defensiveness marked my stage of metamorphustice™ during most of my college years, the Defensive stage.

At its core, the Defensive stage is characterized by resistance. It's the point where awareness of social injustices encounters personal discomfort, giving rise to a range of emotions – anger, guilt, shame, and confusion, to name a few. These emotions can manifest both inwardly and outwardly, creating an internal and external struggle that can feel overwhelming. This stage can evoke personal extremes – especially when confronted with discussions about privilege, discrimination, or systemic biases. Your mind may become a battlefield of conflicting thoughts. On one hand, you may recognize the existence of social injustices, while on the other, you might be struggling to accept your own role in perpetuating or benefiting from these systems. Your newfound awareness may strain relationships with friends, family members, or colleagues who are at different stages of their own social justice journeys. Conversations can become charged with defensiveness or avoidance. The Defensive stage often prompts deep introspection. You might question your own beliefs, biases, and the extent to which you've contributed, knowingly or unknowingly, to societal inequalities.

Imagine finding out new information that contradicts what you have been taught to be true about the world. This doesn't make you a bad person; rather, especially when progressing from the Oblivious stage, you are simply becoming more aware. You might appear to be closed off to certain perspectives because you are simply trying to make sense of conflicting views regarding the world around you. Others will pick up on this and will possibly make their own stories up regarding why you are so conflicted. It is critical to communicate during this stage. Learning about others and their lived experiences without shame, blame, or guilt is the only way you can progress through the Defensive stage. If you don't do this, you may find yourself further manifesting these thoughts into denial, resentment, further blame, and fear. It is also crucial to remember that these feelings, left unchecked, can be paralyzing, leading to inaction or a sense of powerlessness, hindering progress toward social justice reform.

Some individuals respond to discomfort by denying the existence of privilege, systemic oppression, or discrimination altogether. They may argue that these issues are exaggerated or blown out of proportion. This denial often serves as a protective mechanism, allowing them to avoid confronting unsettling truths. By minimizing the problem, they attempt to maintain a sense of personal comfort and innocence. For others, defensiveness takes the form of anger directed at individuals or groups of people. This anger can be toward others or even toward your own identities. This anger can be a defense mechanism often accompanied by phrases like, "Why should I feel guilty for something I didn't do?" or "Why can't they just get over it?" This anger can also be a shame mechanism often accompanied by phrases like, "I must be a bad person because others who look/act/sound like me are bad." People might feel guilty for their own privilege or for not having been aware of these issues sooner. In some cases, individuals become immobilized by their guilt, unsure of how to move forward without feeling overwhelmed. Some individuals avoid conversations about social justice altogether because they fear confrontation or judgment. They may withdraw from such discussions or remain silent even when they witness discrimination. This fear often stems from concerns about being labeled as 'racist', 'sexist', or a multitude of other bias-based terms. They may perceive any critique of their beliefs or actions as a personal attack, leading to defensiveness and avoidance. In the Defensive stage, confirmation bias can intensify. People seek out information that reinforces their existing beliefs while dismissing or discrediting opposing viewpoints. They may surround themselves with like-minded individuals and consume media that aligns with their perspective. This selective exposure serves as a protective mechanism, reinforcing their sense of certainty and shielding them from the discomfort of challenging ideas.

The Defensive stage is not a one-size-fits-all experience. It can manifest in various ways. These manifestations reflect an individual's emotional response to their growing awareness of social injustices. Each response comes with its own set of challenges and potential barriers to personal growth. The Defensive stage is characterized by a delicate balance between self-preservation and the potential for transformation.

The Defensive stage can be a daunting place to find oneself. It's marked by intense emotions, internal conflicts, and external challenges. However, it's also a critical stage of growth on the path toward social justice reform. If you find yourself in the Defensive stage, the most important attribute to build upon when progressing into the next stage of metamorphustice™ is care and concern. Remember that people aren't villains and we are all on our own transformational journey. Ask questions with the intent to understand different perspectives and challenge your own assumptions. Navigating the Defensive stage requires introspection, education, and a willingness to confront discomfort.

If you are helping someone else progress through the Defensive stage, listen without judgment or interruption. Create a safe space for others to express their feelings and concerns. After listening, consider asking for permission to share another perspective that may be different from their own – remembering that it is only through impacting the heart that we can change anyone's mind. While it's essential to challenge harmful biases, avoid confrontational or accusatory language. Focus on facilitating understanding rather than winning an argument. Most importantly within the Defensive stage, remember that personal growth takes time. Be patient and understanding as others navigate their own personal transformation. Supporting others in this stage demands patience and a commitment to the growth of others and ourselves. By fostering a safe and understanding environment, we can help individuals move through the Defensive stage toward greater awareness and personal transformation.

As you journey through this stage, keep in mind that awareness of others' lived experiences without guilt, shame, or blame, is paramount. We cannot change what our ancestors did or didn't do. What we can do, though, is learn about the achievement and missteps of our ancestors so we don't repeat the negative. As Core Principle #1 states, guilt is one of the components that perpetuate prejudice and stigma. Within this, we can also loop in the concept of shame. It is only through genuine curiosity and growth that we can continue social justice reform.

Journal Prompts:

1. Recall a recent situation where you felt defensive or resistant when confronted with a social justice issue. What triggered this defensive response, and what emotions did you experience?

   _____

   _____

   _____

   _____

2. Explore the roles of guilt, shame, and blame in your reactions to social justice topics. Have these emotions been a part of your defensive stance? How have they affected your willingness to engage with these issues?

   _____

   _____

   _____

   _____

3. Reflect on the importance of self-awareness when it comes to addressing defensiveness. How might recognizing your own biases and defense mechanisms help you progress beyond this stage?

   _____

   _____

   _____

   _____

4. Consider your reactions when you encounter ideas or opinions that challenge your existing beliefs. How do you typically respond to differing perspectives, and what impact does this have on constructive dialogue?

_____

_____

_____

5. Explore the impact of defensiveness on your relationships, both personally and professionally. Have you ever faced challenges in your interactions with others due to your defensive stance?

_____

_____

_____

6. Consider the broader implications of the Defensive stage. How can an individual's defensiveness contribute to systemic injustices or perpetuate prejudices in society?

_____

_____

_____

7. Imagine a future where you've progressed beyond the Defensive stage. What actions or strategies can you implement to move forward into a more constructive and open approach to social justice conversations?

_____

_____

_____

Stage 3: Savior

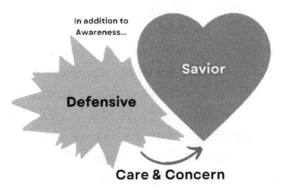

"Seeking to save others can unveil an unconscious belief of superiority."

In the journey of social justice reform, the Savior stage is a pivotal juncture. At this stage, individuals often find themselves compelled to 'save' others whom they perceive as less fortunate or disadvantaged. While their intentions may be noble, there's an underlying aspect to this stage that warrants exploration – the unconscious belief of superiority.

While in college, especially after starting to learn more about the social injustices surrounding so many in our society, I started volunteering at an orphanage in the Dominican Republic. This started because so many of the people around me were going on Spring Break (either partying on a caribbean island or volunteering for a mission trip). Neither of those options seemed particularly aligned to who I was. I knew I wanted to make a difference in the world and I found an organization that organized volunteer trips to an orphanage in the Dominican Republic. Volunteers would either conduct work projects (construction) or teach the children. I was excited to be part of an organization that helped out those 'less fortunate'. Once I arrived, I fell in love with the community. I decided to go back over 20 times in the course of the next 6 years. After my second trip, I made the decision to go on my own rather than through the organization. I felt that my work and funds would be best used for direct support of the orphanage rather than through the organization. I know that I helped many people in the community – but, in reflection, I realize that there was a large part of my decision that was in the Savior mentality. Whether I knew it at the time or not, I thought I was 'saving' the people in the community. This continued into my early teaching career. I went into teaching to 'change the world'. Once I started engaging in my own exploration of social justice (after being isolated from diverse experiences for so long), I had grand plans of making sure the students I taught, whether they were from a societally marginalized population or not, would be aware of the world outside of their bubble. My first few years of teaching consisted of units of study about Africa and Asia. I was so excited to showcase the cultures of the world. What I didn't realize at the time was that I was actually perpetuating the stereotypes that many of my students already had in their minds from mass media and society.

The Savior stage is marked by an ardent desire to help and uplift others. People in this stage genuinely want to make a positive impact on the world, combat injustice, and alleviate suffering. They may engage in various forms of activism, philanthropy, or volunteer work with the intention of making a difference. Individuals in the Savior stage often experience a profound sense of purpose and fulfillment. They feel they are contributing to a more just and equitable society. This stage can be emotionally rewarding, as it aligns with values of social responsibility. From an external perspective, those in the Savior stage may be viewed as altruistic and caring individuals. They are often admired for their dedication to social causes and their willingness to help others in need. This is where the complexities of this stage begin. With so many positive attributes and intentions behind the Savior stage, there's a subtle nuance at play – others may perceive an unconscious sense of superiority beneath their actions.

While individuals in this stage genuinely want to help (I know I did), they may unknowingly hold the assumption that they are somehow better equipped, more knowledgeable, or morally superior to those they aim to save. This sense of superiority can manifest in several ways.

In some cases, individuals from privileged backgrounds may engage in activism or volunteer work in marginalized communities. This has become most popularly referred to as the "White Savior" complex – a belief that they possess the answers and resources to rescue others from their circumstances. It is important to note, though, that the Savior complex, or stage, can be found in all identities of power/privilege. For example, if you identify as a male and want to 'save' the women around you, you might have the "Superman" complex; if you identify as heterosexual and want to 'save' the queer community, you might have the "Straight Hero" complex. Remember, especially within the Savior stage, the intentions are often very positive;

the transformation comes from acknowledging the motivation behind your efforts and uplifting and empowering others' voices toward action rather than 'saving' those you perceive as needing your help.

Seeking to save others can inadvertently imply that one's own light shines brighter or that their potential is greater. This can lead to a subconscious undermining of the capabilities and strengths of the individuals they aim to help. Instead of empowering others to find their own solutions, they may unintentionally perpetuate a sense of dependency. In some instances, the Savior stage can manifest as paternalism, where individuals take on a role akin to a parent, guiding and protecting those they aim to save. While guidance and support are essential, this approach may unintentionally disempower individuals and strip them of agency.

If you find yourself in the Savior stage, the most important attribute to build upon when progressing into the next stage of metamorphustice™ is curiosity. Begin by examining your own motivations and beliefs. Engage in deep self-reflection to uncover any unconscious beliefs or assumptions of superiority that may be guiding your actions. Refer back to the humanization of bias and allow yourself to move through any guilt or shame that you may experience during this reflection process. Learn about the histories, cultures, and experiences of the communities you aim to support. Seek to understand the complexities of the issues at hand from the perspective of those directly affected. Create spaces for individuals to share their stories, perspectives, and solutions. Recognize that they are experts of their own experiences. Instead of imposing solutions, collaborate with communities to identify their needs and work together to address them. Last, and most importantly, be aware that your own privilege and how it shapes your worldview does not negate the experiences and perspectives of others.

If you're in a position to support someone in the Savior stage, it's essential to do so with strong guidance and acknowledging the intentions behind the savioristic tendencies. Encourage individuals to reflect on their motivations and beliefs. Help them uncover any unconscious biases or assumptions of superiority. Some questions to ask that will often help answer this question is, "Why are you the best person to help?" and "Why does this person/group of people need help?" In addition to understanding motivations, consider working towards collaborative approaches that involve community input rather than top-down solutions.

The Savior stage highlights the need for self-awareness and a deeper understanding of the complexities of power, privilege, and equity. As individuals move beyond this stage, they pave the way for more collaborative and effective approaches to creating positive change in the world. In the quest for social justice, recognizing and challenging the unconscious belief of superiority is a transformative step toward meaningful reform. Journal prompts are integral because they encourage introspection, self-awareness, and personal growth. As we continue to transform social justice and lean into curiosity within the next stage of metamorphustice™, this curiosity is mostly directed toward ourselves. Allow yourself to ask, and answer, tough questions that you may not like the answer to. Give yourself grace, knowing that it is only through understanding self that we can understand others, and ultimately unite society.

Journal Prompts:

1. Take some time to write down why you engage in social justice work. What drives your desire to help others? Are there any unconscious assumptions or beliefs about your own superiority in this process?

   _____

   _____

   _____

   _____

2. Consider your biases, whether they are related to race, gender, socio-economic status, or other aspects of identity. Reflect on how these biases might impact the groups you choose to 'save'.

   _____

   _____

   _____

   _____

3. Reflect on the ways in which privilege has shaped your life and experiences. How might your privilege impact your perspective when trying to 'save' others?

   _____

   _____

   _____

   _____

4. Write about a specific experience where you tried to help someone or a community. How did you approach the situation? Did you consider the perspectives and needs of those you were trying to assist?

    _____

    _____

    _____

5. Describe a time when you learned something valuable from someone whose experiences or background were different from your own. How did this experience change your perspective or approach to social justice work?

    _____

    _____

    _____

6. Consider your approach to addressing social issues. Do you tend to dictate solutions, or do you collaborate with communities and individuals to find solutions together? Share your thoughts on these approaches.

    _____

    _____

    _____

7. Think about ways you can progress beyond the Savior stage. What steps can you take to foster more equitable and inclusive practices in your social justice work?

    _____

    _____

    _____

Stage 4: Ally

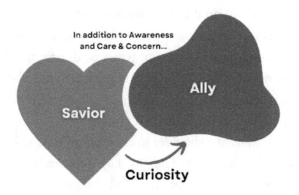

"Sympathy can be what is needed in the moment, but it won't move us to action."

In the journey of social justice reform, the stage of being an Ally has shifted dramatically over the years. Within metamorphustice™, an Ally is someone who sympathizes with the oppressed or marginalized groups, acknowledging their struggles and advocating for justice. An Ally is very similar to a Savior, in that both have high levels of care and concern with sympathy being paramount. However, within the Ally stage, you add on the attribute of curiosity. As a Savior, there is often an assumption of knowing what is best for the marginalized group; whereas, during the Ally stage, curiosity leads to asking more questions to better understand rather than assuming to know what is best for people from marginalized groups.

We all need a shoulder to cry on from time to time. This is the role of Ally. The Ally stage is marked by genuine care and concern for others; it is a stage of sympathy, where individuals begin to ask questions regarding the challenges and injustices faced by marginalized groups. This recognition prompts a desire to take action and is often stymied due to the focus on sympathy rather than empathy. As an Ally, you will often find yourself listening more than speaking. You'll engage in conversations and education to gain a deeper understanding of the experiences and challenges faced by those who are systemically and systematically marginalized.

We have seen a stark increase in this stage – especially on social media. If you have ever scrolled through your social media feed and provided a 'care' emoji or felt an emotional pull toward a post, but didn't necessarily take action regarding the information shared in the post, you might have been in the Ally stage. Again, as shared multiple times, there is no 'bad' stage – we have all probably been at different stages within metamorphustice™ and we will continue to progress and regress through the many stages. Instead, we must recognize the stages we are currently in and work toward progression as much as possible.

While being an Ally is a critical stage of metamorphustice™, there are potential downfalls. It's essential to avoid falling into the trap of performative Allyship, where your actions are driven by a desire to appear virtuous rather than making a genuine impact. This is seen by the social media posts of people sharing a video of them doing something nice for someone else. If the kindness was simply kindness, why is there a need to post/share on social media? This is seen as performative Allyship because it seems to be driven by a desire to portray a certain image to the public. Performative Allies may engage in superficial activism to maintain a positive image without necessarily making a tangible impact. It's essential to recognize that performative Allyship can undermine the very causes you aim to support. Instead of addressing the systemic issues and injustices faced by marginalized communities, this approach may reinforce shallow gestures that ultimately benefit the Ally more than the marginalized group. Relying solely on sympathy and appearing virtuous without transitioning to curiosity and a deeper understanding can limit your effectiveness as an Ally.

If you find yourself in the Ally stage, it is critical to engage in conversations where the stories of marginalized voices are validated without voices from privileged groups dominating the conversation. In order to move into the next stage of metamorphustice™, a level of understanding and empathy is needed, which is only possible within curious conversations.

If you are helping someone else progress from the Ally stage, encourage them to participate in initiatives, campaigns, or events aimed at supporting marginalized communities. By participating in events such as these, the transition from sympathy and passive commitment to empathy and active commitment starts to take hold. Supporting and progressing as an Ally and beyond is a dynamic process that requires commitment, continuous learning, and meaningful action. Remember that awareness, care & concern, and curiosity are all essential attributes within the Ally stage, enabling you to contribute to lasting change and continue social justice reform.

As individuals progress through the stages of metamorphustice™, they develop the capacity to recognize systemic injustices and their own privileges. Allyship is about understanding that sympathy and genuine care for others are the first steps toward curiosity and a deeper understanding of the struggles faced by marginalized communities. In embracing Allyship, individuals align themselves with a broader movement for social change. The journey towards becoming an effective Ally is marked by a growing awareness of the experiences of others, a willingness to learn, and a dedication to contributing to a more just and inclusive world.

Journal Prompts:

1. Write down the different definitions you have heard for the word Ally. Which definitions resonate with you?

   _____

   _____

   _____

   _____

2. Reflect on a time when you first recognized systemic inequities faced by marginalized communities. What sparked your initial curiosity or sympathy?

   _____

   _____

   _____

   _____

3. Think about your online presence. How can you leverage social media or digital platforms to move beyond sympathy and care/concern?

   _____

   _____

   _____

   _____

4. Consider the potential pitfalls of performative Allyship. Have you ever caught yourself engaging in actions primarily for recognition rather than genuine support?

    _____

    _____

    _____

5. Imagine your path forward as you transition away from sympathy, through curiosity, and into empathy. What specific steps can you take to deepen your understanding and Allyship?

    _____

    _____

    _____

6. Think about a peer or friend who is currently in the Ally stage. How can you best support their journey and foster their growth within metamorphustice™?

    _____

    _____

    _____

7. Consider a world where people move beyond the sympathy-based stage of Ally. What are some points of evidence to showcase the move toward empathy rather than sympathy?

    _____

    _____

    _____

Stage 5: Advocate

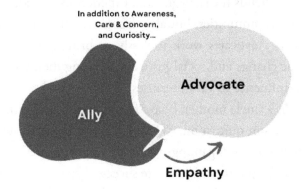

"I will use my breath to speak for those who cannot breathe."

The Advocate stage stands as a powerful and impactful stage. Advocates are individuals who have transitioned from sympathy to empathy, and they utilize their voices and actions to speak up for those whose voices have been silenced or marginalized. At this stage, people understand the need for change and actively engage in advocating for it. The Advocate stage embodies the essence of empathy, where one not only comprehends the struggles and experiences of marginalized communities, but also decides to take an active stance. Advocates work tirelessly to bring about systemic change and social justice by lending their voices and influence to various causes.

As a single mother, I have found myself advocating for my son quite a bit. When I see him being treated unfairly or not gaining access to opportunities that would help him achieve more success, I step in. I'll call the teacher and/or principal (maybe even the superintendent). I'll request a conversation with the coach of a team he plays on. I might even call another parent to try and brainstorm how to resolve a situation that is happening at school. Note that I am still using present-tense when I speak about these examples. I find myself doing this less and less; at the same time, I acknowledge that sometimes it is important for an Advocate to step in and support. An Advocate doesn't wait to be asked to step in; they see something happening to invalidate or minimize someone they care about and they jump in – sometimes without thinking through exactly what to say, how to say it, when to say it, and/or the impact of jumping in. Advocates will often be guided by their concern and empathy so much so that they forget that the most powerful tool within metamorphustice™ is uplifting other voices rather than speaking FOR marginalized communities.

Advocates often act independently, speaking out without waiting to be asked to represent others. They will often find themselves deeply moved by the experiences and stories of marginalized communities, and this passion drives them to advocate for change. Advocates are typically seen as passionate and committed to social justice causes while being vocal, persuasive, and determined in their efforts to bring about change. However, some may perceive Advocates as overly aggressive or confrontational, especially if their advocacy challenges the status quo.

Within the role of Advocate, there are two main struggles to be mindful of. The first potential pitfall of being an Advocate is that their passion can sometimes lead to burnout. The weight of continuously fighting for justice can become overwhelming. At the same time, it is important to note that people from marginalized communities don't get to 'choose' when they are going to think about social injustices because it is simply how their lived experiences translate. Another struggle of the Advocate stage is similar to a struggle within the Savior stage – inadvertently overshadowing the voices of those they are advocating for, unintentionally reinforcing power dynamics. It is critical to ask for permission before speaking up on someone's behalf within the Advocate role. Once permission is granted, action can be taken from an anonymous standpoint to ensure safety (both physical and psychological).

If you find yourself in the Advocate stage, the most important attribute to build upon when progressing into the next stage of metamorphustice™ is empowerment. Rather than speaking on behalf of someone else without permission, consider providing a safe space to allow the person who is being marginalized to speak on their own behalf. Take the time to center the voices of the communities you advocate for. If the space is not safe (which can happen for a variety of reasons), ask for permission to advocate on their behalf before jumping into the role of Advocate. It is also important to notate which groups you find yourself advocating for – are there similarities across identities? By exploring the identities that you advocate for most often, you will be able to uncover any potential biases that you may have; allowing you to understand them and move forward without allowing your biases to dictate how you communicate with others.

If you are helping someone else progress from the Advocate stage, encourage them to uplift marginalized voices rather than solely speaking for others. Consider facilitating opportunities for different voices to be heard. The emotional toll of advocacy can be substantial. Advocates may grapple with burnout, compassion fatigue, or trauma as they immerse themselves in the struggles of marginalized communities. When working with fellow Advocates, remember to offer emotional support and encouragement as much as possible to help navigate the emotional toll of the Advocate stage. Self-care and a support network are essential for sustaining their efforts.

The Advocate stage signifies a profound commitment to justice and social change. Advocates, through fearlessly speaking out, often pave the way for progress and inspire others to join the cause. Advocates leverage their voices, resources, and influence to address pressing societal issues, and in doing so, they contribute to the betterment of communities, institutions, and societies as a whole. Advocacy is a testament to the enduring power of empathy and the belief that collective action can bring about a more just and inclusive world.

Journal Prompts:

1. Reflect on a time when you were inspired by an Advocate's work or message. What about their advocacy resonated with you? How did it influence your perspective or actions?

   _____

   _____

   _____

   _____

2. Consider the challenges and emotional toll that advocacy can entail. How do you personally manage the potential challenges and maintain your well-being while advocating for change?

   _____

   _____

   _____

   _____

3. Explore your own role as an Advocate or your potential to become one. Are there specific issues or causes you are passionate about advocating for? What steps can you take to amplify your advocacy efforts?

   _____

   _____

   _____

   _____

4. Have you ever felt that your advocacy overshadowed the voices of the marginalized group(s) you were advocating for? How can you ensure this doesn't happen?

    _____

    _____

    _____

    _____

5. In what ways have you seen people advocate in society? What has been successful? Why?

    _____

    _____

    _____

    _____

6. How do you see being able to transition from speaking on behalf of marginalized voices to empowering them to speak for themselves?

    _____

    _____

    _____

    _____

7. Reflect on your journey as an Advocate. What's the most critical lesson you've learned along the way?

    _____

    _____

    _____

    _____

Stage 6: Co-Conspirator

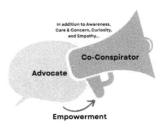

"'You cannot heal what you do not reveal."

Co-Conspirators are what many people refer to as the pinnacle of social justice reform. Co-Conspirators are individuals who recognize their privilege and leverage it to amplify the voices of marginalized communities. This stage represents a progression beyond mere advocacy or allyship, as Co-Conspirators actively empower others to speak up and use their voices to challenge systemic inequities. They move beyond simply not being discriminatory themselves and being anti-discriminatory when reflecting on the actions of others – ensuring that discriminatory behavior does not happen in their presence or in their circles of influence. They actively work to eliminate discrimination. They are often reactive, responding to injustices as they arise in their presence but not necessarily seeking them out proactively, a characteristic that distinguishes them from reaching the final stage of metamorphustice™.

The last ten years of my career in the school systems was mostly in this stage of Co-Conspiratorship. When I saw unjust behaviors, actions, or policies, I found myself speaking up and uplifting the voices of those most affected by the discrimination. I also recognize now that I wasn't always aware of the discriminatory behaviors until they were happening right in front of me, or they were brought to my attention. Again, referring back to Core Principle #7, we don't know what we don't know, and I was a testament to that. At the same time, as we have mentioned before, this can't be used as an excuse to not act. Within Co-Conspiratorship, there are times when obliviousness can creep into the situation – unknowingly supporting and empowering only the identities that are publicly being oppressed or marginalized.

The Co-Conspirator stage signifies a commitment to social justice that transcends passive awareness or sympathy. Co-Conspirators acknowledge their privilege and actively work to address social injustices, even if they themselves aren't directly impacted. They use their platform, resources, and influence to uplift the voices of those who are systematically oppressed or marginalized and they respond to instances of injustice by taking action in the moment.

Co-Conspirators invest time in learning about systemic oppression, intersectionality, and the lived experiences of marginalized groups. They work collaboratively with impacted communities and recognize that true change requires collaboration and consult with those directly affected to guide their social justice efforts. They also actively support initiatives that redistribute resources, whether through donations, fundraising, or volunteering, to address systemic disparities.

Throughout history, there have been inspiring examples of Co-Conspirators who played pivotal roles in advancing the cause of justice. One prominent illustration is the Civil Rights Movement in the United States. White-presenting individuals who joined forces with black leaders during this era ex-emplified Co-Conspiratorship. They recognized their privilege and stood in solidarity with the struggle for racial equality, advocating for civil rights and challenging segregation.

While Co-Conspirators play a vital role in social justice movements, their work is not without challenges. Co-Conspirators may face skepticism or criticism from both within their own communities and those they aim to support. Some may question their motives or authenticity, emphasizing the importance of navigating such challenges with humility and resistance. Also, by waiting for a situation to be brought to the forefront of a Co-Conspirators world, they risk perpetuating a reactive approach to social justice. Their work might be seen as sporadic, inconsistent, or too narrowly focused on one particular identity group, potentially leading to challenges in creating lasting change. Co-Conspirators must continuously evaluate their actions to avoid falling into this by striving for genuine impact rather than mere appearances. It is critical to right all social injustices and not just the unjust behaviors that most impact you personally. Co-Conspirators also often grapple with the balance between taking action and allowing impacted communities to lead. It's essential to recognize when to step back and when to step in, with the ultimate goal of long-term change.

If you find yourself in the Co-Conspirator stage, it is critical to remember Core Principle #5, "Every issue counts". Oppression occurs in many levels of society and we must take action to ensure that everyone is seen, welcomed, valued, and heard. This means going beyond what we experience personally and what we witness in the moment. We must be proactive when looking for populations that need more access, more agency, and more presence. It is important to shift focus from addressing individual instances of injustice to working on systemic change. Continuously assess the impact of your interventions and actions; leverage your privileges to support marginalized groups and advance justice.

If you are helping someone else progress from the Co-Conspirator stage, acknowledge and amplify their actions toward being anti-discriminatory. Celebrate their willingness to take a stand in the moment and encourage them to continue moving toward more proactive approaches. The final stages of metamorphustice™ can be emotionally taxing – consider building a support network of like-minded individuals. Groups of people have the ability to impact systemic change much more effectively with a greater chance of long-term impact.

Co-Conspirators have built upon attributes of the previous stages of metamorphustice™. They have a level of awareness, demonstrate genuine care and concern, are curious about the lived experiences of others, show empathy, and work toward empowerment. True transformation and accountability – leading to sustainable change – occurs in the final stage.

Journal Prompts:

1. Share a story of a time when your immediate response as a Co-Conspirator led to a positive change or resolution. How did it affect the situation and the individuals involved?

    _____

    _____

    _____

    _____

2. Consider the balance between reacting to injustices and seeking them out proactively. How can you develop a more proactive approach to your social justice reform work?

    _____

    _____

    _____

    _____

3. In your journey to become more proactive, what are the most significant areas of systemic change you are passionate about addressing?

    _____

    _____

    _____

    _____

4. Reflect on a specific instance where you encountered resistance or backlash while taking action as a Co-Conspirator. How did you navigate these challenges, and what did you learn from the experience?

_____

_____

_____

5. Consider a situation where your reactivity as a Co-Conspirator may have led to unintended consequences or misunderstandings. What did you learn from that experience, and how can you prevent similar situations in the future?

_____

_____

_____

6. Reflect on the challenges Co-Conspirators face. How can you navigate these challenges in your own metamorphustice™?

_____

_____

_____

7. Explore the concept of global Co-Conspiratorship. Are there international social justice issues that resonate with you? How can you contribute to global equity and inclusion?

_____

_____

_____

Stage 7: CHANGEmaker

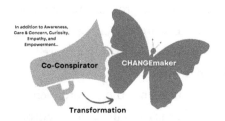

"'Be the change you wish to see
in the world." -Gandhi

We have arrived at the final stage of metamorphustice™ - the stage of CHANGEmaker. This stage represents the culmination of a long and often challenging process, where individuals have progressed from being oblivious to embody the spirit of social change and actively seeking opportunities to dismantle systemic injustices without waiting for issues to arise. CHANGEmakers are individuals who have internalized the principles of social justice and make it a part of their daily lives. They understand that social change is an ongoing commitment and actively look for opportunities to address systemic injustices. CHANGEmakers are driven by the conviction that they can contribute to creating a more just, equitable, and inclusive world.

As a reminder, the word change within CHANGEmaker is capitalized for a purpose. In addition to being the final stage of metamorphustice™, the CHANGE within CHANGEmaker is an acronym for the values that must be adhered to in order to ensure transformational change within social justice reform.

The C stands for Commitment, serving as a driving force that propels individuals through the various stages of metamorphustice™. Without commitment, the process may stagnate, and the growth and transformation that might come with each stage might remain unrealized. The commitment to transformation is essential because it signifies a conscious decision to move forward and not regress. It encourages individuals to confront the inherent challenges and discomfort that come with understanding and addressing complex issues related to justice, equity, diversity, and inclusion. This commitment not only accelerates personal growth, but also benefits communities and organizations as they move toward a more just and inclusive world. Commitment involves recognizing that the process is ongoing and that each stage serves as a stepping stone to the next. It implies a willingness to persevere and continually seek opportunities for growth and learning. A commitment to the process of social justice tranformation enables individuals to remain resilient in the face of obstacles, whether internal or external. Moreover, commitment aligns with the concept that lasting change requires ongoing effort. Social justice issues are multifaceted and dynamic, and tackling them effectively demands sustained dedication. Commitment encourages individuals to keep moving forward, embracing justice, equity, diversity, and inclusion as lifelong pursuits rather than short-term goals. In essence, commitment within metamorphustice™ is the catalyst for personal, societal, and organizational transformation. It propels individuals forward, motivates them to act on their convictions, and ultimately fosters a world where everyone can fluorish.

The H stands for Heart-Focused, emphasizing compassion, empathy, and genuine concern for others.

This perspective recognizes that social justice transformation is fundamentally a human endeavor, built
on understanding, respect, and love. It underscores
the importance of fostering an environment where
individuals are valued, welcomed, seen, and heard.
The heart-focused approach encourages deep introspection, prompting individuals to explore their own
emotions and biases. It promotes self-awareness, as it is
only through understanding one's own heart that true
empathy and compassion can be extended to others.
This self-reflection serves as a foundation for authentic
connections and relationships. As Core Principle #4
states, we must start with impacting the heart, which
ultimately changes the mind. In the context of social
justice, a heart-focused approach inspires individuals to not only recognize and address the struggles of
others but to actively advocate for change. It compels
people to take action out of love and concern for the
well-being of all, motivating them to fight for justice
and inclusion. Moreover, a heart-focused perspective
within metamorphustice™ promotes unity rather than
division. It fosters collaboration, cooperation, and
solidarity among diverse groups, acknowledging that a
shared commitment to social justice can bridge divides
and lead to more profound and lasting change. At its
core, the heart-focused approach speaks to the mor-
al compass that guides individuals on their journey
through the stages of metamorphustice™. It challenges

people to lead with their hearts, understanding that genuine transformation comes from a place of love, acceptance, and an unwavering dedication to a more just and equitable world.

The A stands for Accountability, which creates a framework for individuals to take ownership of their actions, words, and beliefs. It holds people responsible for their role in perpetuating or challenging social injustices, ensuring that they actively contribute to positive change. In the context of social justice, accountability also requires self-reflection and introspection, prompting individuals to examine their biases, prejudices, and behaviors. It compels them to acknowledge their privilege and recognize where they have fallen short in supporting marginalized groups. Accountability also extends to a broader level, where it demands that organizations, institutions, and society as a whole recognize and address systemic inequalities. This approach ensures that those in positions of power are held responsible for their policies and practices, leading to more equitable and inclusive structures. Furthermore, accountability fosters trust and transparency. It encourages open dialogue, accountability partnerships, and the sharing of resources and information to drive social justice initiatives forward. Accountability is the driving force behind lasting change. It propels individuals to move beyond passive awareness or performative allyship and take concrete, measurable steps to challenge injustice. It forms the foundation for sustainable progress and a more equitable society.

The N stands for Networking, which creates connections and alliances. In the context of social justice, networking allows individuals to join forces, collaborate, and share resources, amplifying their collective impact. These connections enable the spread of ideas, resources, and strategies to challenge and change oppressive systems. Networking also facilitates a cross-pollination of perspectives. When individuals from diverse backgrounds come together, they bring unique experiences and knowledge, enriching the dialogue and understanding of complex issues. It opens the door for a wider range of voices to be heard and valued. Moreover, networking is a source of support and solidarity. In the face of adversity, individuals can turn to their network for emotional and strategic assistance. It creates a safety net and a sense of community, where like-minded people can find encouragement and guidance. At a systemic level, networking bridges the gap between different sectors, organizations, and institutions. This interconnectedness can lead to the creation of new policies, initiatives, and frameworks for social justice, ultimately fostering a more inclusive and equitable society. By building and nurturing a robust network, individuals contribute to a powerful force for change within the metamorphustice™ framework. It harnesses collective energy and resources to address, challenge, and dismantle the structures that perpetuate social injustices.

The G stands for Genuine by underpinning authenticity, trust, and integrity. Being genuine means consistently aligning one's own actions and words with their beliefs and values, particularly when advocating for social justice and equity. Authenticity is essential because it ensures that the commitment to change is sincere and not motivated by superficial or insincere intentions. Genuine individuals approach social justice with an honest and transparent mindset, which fosters trust among their peers and within the community. Integrity, another facet of being genuine, involves staying true to one's principles even when it's challenging or inconvenient. This principle is vital in the context of social justice, as it implies a steadfast dedication to creating a more equitable and inclusive society. Being genuine also helps in building bridges and forming connections with others. Authenticity in intentions and interactions fosters meaningful relationships, which are crucial when working together to advance the cause of social justice. Overall, genuinity ensures that those who are part of this transformation are resolute, reliable, and honest in their efforts to challenge and reshape the systems that perpetuate social inequalities.

The E stands for Empowerment, the ultimate goal of transformation. Embodying the concept of agency and autonomy, empowerment encourages individuals to take an active role in shaping their communities. Empowerment is vital because it encourages individuals to participate, engage, and collaborate with others in the pursuit of a more just and equitable society. By empowering individuals to become CHANGEmakers, the metamorphustice™ framework ensures that the transformation toward social justice is a collective effort. Empowerment also emphasizes the significance of sharing power and influence, particularly with marginalized and oppressed groups. It recognizes that true social justice cannot be achieved without equitable distribution of resources and opportunities, allowing everyone to have a voice and agency in decision-making processes. Additionally, empowerment is crucial for breaking down hierarchical structures and challenging systems of oppressions. It allows individuals to become active in dismantling oppressive systems and fostering more inclusive, diverse, and equitable communities. Furthermore, empowerment bolsters the sense of self-worth and confidence among those who work toward social justice. It acknowledges that everyone has the potential to make a difference, encouraging them to embrace their agency and effect change. In essence, empowerment propels individuals to realize their power, share it with others, and collectively work toward a world where social justice, equity, and inclusivity thrive.

Becoming a CHANGEmaker is a profound and life-changing experience. It's a stage marked by a constant awareness of social issues, a deep commitment to addressing them, and a proactive approach to making a difference. CHANGEmakers are not passive observers, but rather active participants in the ongoing struggle for social justice. CHANGEmakers often find themselves engaging in a variety of actions, both big and small, to drive change. They may participate in grassroots movements, work toward policy reforms, and collaborate with like-minded individuals and organizations. Their experiences are shaped by a sense of purpose, the drive to create impact, and a willingness to take risks in the pursuit of justice.

CHANGEmakers are often perceived as passionate, driven, and relentless in their pursuit for social justice. Others see them as individuals who not only talk the talk, but walk the walk. They even go one step further than simply walking the walk – by seeing results from their actions. They are often admired for their unwavering commitment and the tangible impact they create in their communities and beyond. However, CHANGEmakers may also be perceived as intense or radical by some. Their dedication to challenging the status quo and their willingness to confront systemic injustices can be unsettling for those who prefer the comfort of conformity. However, CHANGEmakers are not deterred by these perceptions; they understand that pushing boundaries is often necessary for real change to occur.

While being a CHANGEmaker is a powerful and transformative stage, it is not without its challenges and limitations. CHANGEmakers can experience burnout due to the emotional and physical toll of seeking justice reform. The constant exposure to social injustices can be emotionally draining, leading to compassion fatigue. It is important to note, though, that the fatigue experienced by CHANGEmakers is not to be compared to the battle that people from marginalized groups must endure within society on a daily basis. Additionally, CHANGEmakers may face resistance from individuals or systems invested in maintaining the status quo. They can encounter pushback from those who are uncomfortable with change or who perceive their actions as threats to their own privilege and power. It is often people within the Defensive stage that are the biggest challenge to CHANGEmakers.

Maintaining the stage of CHANGEmaker within metamorphustice™ is a challenging yet deeply rewarding endeavor. It requires a holistic approach, ensuring that personal well-being, a sense of community, and continuous self-improvement are at the forefront of an individual's efforts. CHANGEmakers often pour their hearts and souls into social justice work. To prevent burnout and maintain their effectiveness, they must prioritize self-care. This may include setting boundaries, practicing mindfulness, and engaging in activities that bring joy and relaxation. Acknowledging the emotional toll of social justice work is crucial. CHANGEmakers need to make their mental health a priority, seeking therapy or counseling when needed. It's also essential to develop healthy coping mechanisms to navigate the emotional challenges that may arise. Balancing social justice work with a personal life is a constant juggling act. CHANGEmakers benefit from recognizing that taking care of themselves ultimately enhances their advocacy work. A support system is also invaluable. By connecting with a community that provides encouragement, shared experiences, and emotional support, relationships can foster resilience and sustain motivation. Lastly, staying informed about emerging issues, progressive strategies, and intersectional approaches is essential to maintaining efficacy. The stage of CHANGEmaker is consistently changing and evolving – the ability to adapt ensures relevance and impact in an ever-changing world.

In addition to maintaining your own stage of metamorphustice™, supporting a fellow CHANGEmaker is a meaningful endeavor with nuanced opportunities. Recognize and affirm the dedication, effort, and sacrifice that CHANGEmakers invest in their work. A simple acknowledgement can go a long way in motivating and validating their efforts. Lend a compassionate ear, providing a safe space to express their feelings and frustrations. Empathetic listening can be cathartic. One of the most effective ways to support a CHANGEmaker is by actively engaging in social justice work alongside them. Collaborative efforts not only amplify the impact, but also foster a sense of solidarity. Consider helping to amplify their message by providing a platform. Share their content, engage with their campaigns, and encourage your networks to do the same. By nurturing the well-being of fellow CHANGEmakers and actively participating in their efforts, individuals can contribute to the sustainability and impact of social justice reform.

In the final stage of metamorphustice™, individuals who have become CHANGEmakers have internalized the principles of social justice, transforming themselves into catalysts for lasting change and signifying a deep commitment to social justice, active leadership, and a proactive stance in fostering JEDI principles. They actively seek opportunities to address systemic injustices, uphold the values of justice, equity, diversity, and inclusion, and embody the belief that a better world is possible. CHANGEmakers can inspire others to join the movement and work collectively to create a more just and equitable society. Remember that the path is not linear, and individuals may navigate these stages at their own pace. Whether you find yourself in the earlier stages of Savior or Ally or the advanced stage of being a CHANGEmaker, your commitment to social justice is a powerful force for change. Together, we can continue the work of transforming social justice.

Journal Prompts:

1. Reflect on a time when you were inspired by a CHANGEmaker. What aspects of their work motivated you to take action?

   _____

   _____

   _____

   _____

2. How do you personally embody the core values of CHANGE (Commitment, Heart-Focused, Accountability, Networking, Genuine, Empowerment)?

   _____

   _____

   _____

   _____

3. Consider the challenges and limitations you've encountered (or envision encountering) as a CHANGEmaker. How have you managed burnout or resistance from others?

   _____

   _____

   _____

   _____

4. Describe a project or initiative that you are currently involved in that aligns with the CHANGEmaker stage. What are your goals, and how do you intend to achieve them?

_____

_____

_____

5. How do you maintain your commitment to social justice work while ensuring a healthy work-life balance and self-care?

_____

_____

_____

6. Consider how you can collaborate with other CHANGEmakers to amplify your collective impact. What opportunities exist for synergy in your social justice efforts?

_____

_____

_____

7. Reflect on your long-term vision as a CHANGEmaker. What kind of societal transformation do you hope to achieve, and what steps will you take to realize that vision?

_____

_____

_____

_____

Becoming Pollinators of Change

How can I transform
as an individual?

_____
_____
_____
_____
_____
_____
_____
_____
_____
_____
_____
_____
_____
_____
_____
_____
_____
_____
_____
_____
_____
_____
_____
_____
_____

In the closing section of this social justice transformation, we delve into the concept of becoming a Pollinator of CHANGE. This concept carries with it a profound responsibility to create ripples of transformation in society beyond our individual experiences.

Becoming a Pollinator of CHANGE means recognizing that passive awareness and sympathy are no longer sufficient. It's about taking deliberate and strategic action to bring about positive shifts in your community and society at large. The time for inaction has passed, and it's crucial to identify tangible steps you can take to effect change.

Curiosity remains an essential ingredient in our transformation towards becoming a Pollinator of CHANGE. It's about continuously seeking knowledge, understanding, and perspectives that differ from your own. Embrace the idea that learning is a lifelong endeavor and that your curiosity can spark conversations and innovations that lead to transformative outcomes.

Guilt, shame, and blame are blocks to true transformation. As a Pollinator of CHANGE, it's crucial to let go of these negative emotions and focus on productive and constructive actions. Acknowledge that while you may not be responsible for the past, you have the power to shape a more equitable future.

Our society is complex, and issues of justice and equity are rarely binary. To be an effective Pollinator of CHANGE, engage in open, inclusive, and nonjudgmental discussions that consider diverse perspectives. Embrace the gray areas and the nuances of social issues, as this is where transformative solutions often emerge.

As a Pollinator of CHANGE, part of your role is to inspire and empower others to engage in meaningful conversations about social justice. Facilitate discussions, share resources, and lead by example to create a network of other people committed to making a difference.

Recognize the importance of psychological safety in fostering a sense of belonging for all individuals. Encourage open dialogue, active listening, and respectful interactions in your personal and professional spheres. When people feel safe to express themselves, true transformation can occur. Disspelling the misconception that psychological safety equates to weakness is essential. In reality, creating a safe and inclusive environment enhances performance, innovation, and productivity. Embrace this concept and advocate for it within your workplace and community.

Self-discovery is critical for growth and continued learning. Utilize the journal prompts provided throughout this book. Journaling can also help you track your progress, clarify your goals, and gain deeper insights into your journey.

Ultimately, the legacy we leave behind is a testament to the love, compassion, and positive impact we've shared with the world. As a Pollinator of CHANGE, strive to leave a legacy that reflects your commitment to creating a more just and equitable society.

Learning through courses, training, and conversation groups provides space for collective learning and continued discovery. Engaging with others who share your passion for change can amplify your impact and broaden your horizons. Consider joining the book club discussing metamorphustice™ (provided at no additional cost for purchasing your copy of Metamorphustice™) by sharing your information at this QR Code – you will be added to an email list to get updates on the next cohort. The direct link is: https://us2consulting.com/metamorphustice-booktalk/

In closing, embracing the role of a Pollinator of CHANGE requires a commitment to continuous growth, learning, and action. It involves acknowledging the interconnectedness of our lives and recognizing the potential for positive influence within our spheres of influence. By taking these steps, you can be a catalyst for lasting transformation and justice in society.

Journal Prompts:

1. Consider the role of curiosity in your ongoing transformation. What topics, perspectives, or voices will you actively seek out to broaden your understanding of social justice issues?

_____

_____

_____

_____

2. How will you actively work to remove guilt, shame, and blame from your approach to social justice reform? What strategies will you employ to stay focused on productive actions?

_____

_____

_____

_____

3. Explore your willingness to engage in discussions that embrace diverse perspectives and challenge notions of right and wrong. How can you contribute to a more inclusive dialogue on complex issues?

_____

_____

_____

_____

4. If you choose to participate in specialized training, outline your goals and intentions. How will this learning enhance your impact as a Pollinator of CHANGE?

_____

_____

_____

5. Consider the benefits of joining or forming a book club or conversation group focused on social justice. How can you encourage open dialogue and learning within your chosen community?

_____

_____

_____

6. Reflect on your role in inspiring and supporting others to engage in social justice conversations and actions. What steps will you take to become a positive influencer in your network?

_____

_____

_____

7. Use your journal as a tool for ongoing reflection. How have your perspectives and actions evolved throughout your transformation? What milestones have you reached and what goals remain?

_____

_____

_____

_____

How can I transform
as a family member?

All of us are members of a family – whether it be a biological family, a chosen family, or a friend family. A Pollinator of CHANGE within a family setting embodies the principles of the metamorphustice™ framework and extends their transformative approach to their immediate circle. In this context, such individuals play a critical role in fostering understanding, empathy, and equity within the family unit.

Pollinators of CHANGE actively listen to family members, seeking to understand their experiences, perspectives, and emotions. They create a safe space for open dialogue. They set an example of empathy and compassion, demonstrating how to acknowledge and validate each family member's feelings and experiences. Pollinators of CHANGE within a family setting have a unique advantage of having a lifetime of memories and experiences to reflect upon. Within families, we learn each other's triggers and 'magic moments' and learn how to navigate difficult conversations and topics with those in our family units, inspiring family members to self-reflect and foster personal growth and transformation.

Being a Pollinator of CHANGE in a family setting is not without its challenges, as well. Different generations within a family may have varying levels of openness to change, often due to lived experiences that other generations may not be able to relate to. Some family members may fear that addressing social justice issues could disrupt family harmony and Pollinators of CHANGE might be uncertain about how to approach discussions or enact change within the family.

To move through metamorphustice™ with family members, there are a few tips to consider. First, start with empathy. Approach conversations with empathy, focusing on understanding your family members' experiences and concerns. Create spaces for open dialogue, where family members can express their thoughts and feelings without judgment. Model the behavior you wish to see in your family. Be consistent in your commitment to social justice values. Most importantly, be patient. Understand that change takes time, and not all family members will progress at the same pace.

By embodying the Pollinator of CHANGE role within the family, individuals can gradually transform their immediate environment, promoting understanding, inclusion, and empathy among family members. This, in turn, contributes to a more just and equitable society.

Journal Prompts:

1. How has your family background influenced your beliefs and perspectives regarding social justice issues?

    _____

    _____

    _____

    _____

2. Reflect on a moment when a family member's perspective challenged your own. How did you respond? Would you respond differently after reading Metamorphustice™?

    _____

    _____

    _____

    _____

3. What social justice topics do you believe are most important to address within your family? How will you start?

    _____

    _____

    _____

    _____

4. How can you create a safe space for social justice discussions within your family?

5. Consider a family member who might benefit from more understanding or support in their social justice transformation. How can you provide this?

6. Share a recent incident or conversation in which you successfully encouraged empathy and inclusivity within your family.

7. Imagine your ideal family environment with respect to social justice. What steps can you take to move closer to that vision?

Consider
this question

'How can I transform
as an educator?

All of us have been impacted by the educational system. Our formative years were spent learning – from curriculum, teachers, fellow students, and other adults who influenced us. A Pollinator of CHANGE within an educational setting is referring to those currently in an educational environment – as a teacher, instructional assistant, administrator, and/or Board of Education member. Anyone who has the ability to impact how and what our students are taught can be a Pollinator of CHANGE within education.

Pollinators of CHANGE within education advocate for curriculum that reflects diverse perspectives and histories, ensuring that all students see themselves, and others, accurately represented. They prioritize empathy and actively seek to understand their students' experiences, fostering a sense of belonging. They are committed to addressing biases, privileges, and systemic inequalities within the education system, promoting awareness and growth. Pollinators of CHANGE in education work to ensure that all students have equal access to educational opportunities and resources. Lastly, they empower students to become CHANGEmakers, inspiring them to proactively address social justice issues.

Working as a Pollinator of CHANGE within education may also encounter several barriers. First, a lack of training in addressing social justice issues often leads to a lack of foundational knowledge and

common understanding. Without a common understanding and/or lack of knowledge, many constituents
will script their own narrative for the purpose and vision of the work – often incorrectly casting a polariz-
ing viewpoint. Without a clear focus on social justice
in our school settings, some policies and practices may
perpetuate inequities and biases. In addition to why
and how we address social justice issues, the discussion of WHAT we teach (curriculum and resources)
can also serve as a significant barrier. Educational cur-
ricula, although improving, often lack diversity and
representation.

To move through metamorphustice™ with students and other educational constituents, there are
a few tips to consider (some of which are similar to
working with family members). It is critical to push
for changes at the institutional level by advocating for
curricular shifts, inclusive policies, and equity-focused
programs. Consider providing mentorship and support for students who want to take active roles in social
justice reform. Most importantly, commit to your own
continuous learning and growth, staying informed
about social justice issues and sharing your knowledge through transforming your own practices as an
educator.

By embodying the role of a Pollinator of CHANGE
as an educator, individuals can significantly contribute
to transforming educational institutions, promoting

equity, and fostering a more inclusive and empathetic learning environment. This process leads to better educational outcomes and prepares students to actively participate in building a just and equitable society.

Journal Prompts:

1. Reflect on your own educational journey. How have your experiences influenced your commitment to social justice within education?

   _____

   _____

   _____

   _____

2. Describe a moment when a student's perspective on social justice issues challenged your own. How did you respond?

   _____

   _____

   _____

   _____

3. Identify areas within your educational institution that require changes to promote inclusivity and equity. What steps can you take to initiate these changes?

   _____

   _____

   _____

   _____

4. How can you create a safe space for students to discuss
   social justice issues? What resources and strategies will
   you employ?

   _____

   _____

   _____

   _____

5. What actions can you take to ensure that your curriculum
   reflects diverse voices, experiences, and histories?

   _____

   _____

   _____

   _____

6. Reflect on your response to resistance or challenges
   you've encountered in promoting social justice within
   education. How might you address these issues
   differently in the future?

   _____

   _____

   _____

   _____

7. Imagine the future of education within the realm of
   social justice. How can you contribute to this vision, and
   what steps will you take to realize it?

   _____

   _____

   _____

   _____

Consider
this question

How can I transform as
a community member?

_____
_____
_____
_____
_____
_____
_____
_____
_____
_____
_____
_____
_____
_____
_____
_____
_____
_____
_____
_____
_____
_____
_____
_____
_____
_____
_____

We all belong to a community – whether it is a neighborhood community, a work community, a virtual community, or a community of like-minded individuals within an organization or association. A Pollinator of CHANGE within a community is dedicated to ensuring that everyone is seen, heard, welcome, and valued.

Most importantly, Pollinators of CHANGE within a community empower fellow community members to have a voice and play an active role in decision-making processes. They strive to reduce disparities in resources, opportunities, and outcomes within the community and work to bridge gaps among diverse groups to promote unity and cooperation. Lastly, they lead by example, fostering collaboration and teamwork amongst community members to address challenges collectively.

Being a Pollinator of CHANGE within the community also encounters several barriers. Starting at the community level typically gains a lot of attention – this can be good or bad. By drawing attention, not only can you gain followers and the support of like-minded individuals, you can also attract the attention of people who don't appreciate your message. Many of the murders of CHANGEmakers from our past started as Pollinators of CHANGE at the community level. Existing power dynamics (often rooted in systemic oppression and privilege) can make change efforts difficult – and dangerous.

To move through metamorphustice™ with the community, there are a few tips to consider. Engage community members in open dialogues and information-sharing about social justice issues. Pool resources, including time, skills, and knowledge, to work on social justice projects together. Organize educational events and initiatives to increase awareness and understanding of social justice. Work on collaborative projects that promote inclusivity, equity, and positive community change. Lastly, provide a platform for community members to share their experiences, insights, and solutions.

By embodying the role of a Pollinator of CHANGE within the community, individuals can significantly contribute to creating a more equitable, inclusive, and empowered community. This process fosters unity, respect, and positive change, making the community a place where all members can thrive and work together to address social justice challenges.

Journal Prompts:

1. Reflect on your personal connection to the community. How does your relationship with the community influence your commitment to social justice and change?

   _____

   _____

   _____

   _____

2. Identify key social justice issues in your community that need attention. How can you raise awareness about these issues?

   _____

   _____

   _____

   _____

3. Consider a time when you encountered resistance from community members during a social justice initiative. How did you handle the situation, and what did you learn from it?

   _____

   _____

   _____

   _____

4. Share a story of a community member who inspired you with their commitment to social justice. What qualities or actions did they exhibit?

    _____

    _____

    _____

    _____

5. Reflect on the community's diversity. How can this diversity be harnessed as a strength in addressing social justice?

    _____

    _____

    _____

    _____

6. Consider potential obstacles to change in your community. How can you strategize to overcome these challenges?

    _____

    _____

    _____

    _____

7. Imagine the ideal community you would like to create. What values and principles would guide this vision, and how can you work toward it?

    _____

    _____

    _____

    _____

Consider
this question

How can I transform
as a leader?

_____
_____
_____
_____
_____
_____
_____
_____
_____
_____
_____
_____
_____
_____
_____
_____
_____
_____
_____
_____
_____
_____
_____
_____
_____
_____
_____
_____

Pollinator of CHANGE in a leadership role is one of the most impactful opportunities for sustainable change and a shift in policies that guide an organization. This role is a visionary and inclusive leader committed to fostering a culture of social justice, equity, and transformation.

Leaders who serve as Pollinators of CHANGE inspire their team with a clear vision of a socially just and equitable future. They promote diversity, inclusion, and equity with their team, valuing every member's unique perspectives. Leaders who serve as Pollinators of CHANGE are empathetic and in tune with the emotions of their team members, fostering an environment of trust and openness. They hold themselves and their team accountable for their actions and decisions, ensuring alignment with social justice principles. They facilitate collaboration, ensuring that team members work together effectively to address social justice issues and drive change by initiating and supporting initiatives that contribute to social justice and transformation.

Serving as a leader committed to social justice and transformation may also encounter various challenges. Balancing the diverse opinions and values of a team can be complex. Depending on whether the organization is privately or publicly run, this team can expand into the community of public shareholders (if publicly traded). Depending on the level of leadership, existing organizational culture may not support or align with social justice initiatives. For example, mid-managers serve as leaders of their departments/teams; however, they often don't have the ability to shift organizational policies. This can serve as a very difficult piece to navigate and leads us back to the idea of empowerment within all levels of an organization.

To move through metamorphustice™ while leading a team, there are a few invitations to consider. First, include diverse voices in decision-making processes and ensure team members' perspectives are valued and considered when making decisions. Prioritize emotional intelligence and establish open channels for communication and feedback. Champion social justice issues and create policies that promote equity and inclusion. Lastly, invest in the development of team members and team initiatives – provide training and set specific goals that align to the overall mission and vision of the organization. Be sure to track progress and hold all members of the team, including yourself, accountable.

Being a Pollinator of CHANGE in a leadership role is transformative, fostering a culture of social justice, equity, and inclusion. By embracing this role, leaders can inspire positive change and empower their teams to work collaboratively toward a more just and equitable future.

Journal Prompts:

1. Reflect on your leadership style. How can you incorporate the principles of social justice, equity, and transformation into your leadership approach?

    _____

    _____

    _____

    _____

2. Share a story of a time when you successfully led your team toward a social justice initiative. What strategies did you employ, and what was the outcome?

    _____

    _____

    _____

    _____

3. Consider a situation where you faced resistance from team members regarding a proposed change related to social justice. How did you address the resistance, and what did you learn from the experience?

    _____

    _____

    _____

    _____

4. Reflect on your team's current composition. How diverse and inclusive is it, and what steps can you take to enhance diversity and inclusion?

    _____
    _____
    _____
    _____

5. Share a leadership role model who has inspired your commitment to social justice. What qualities or actions of this role model do you admire and aim to emulate?

    _____
    _____
    _____
    _____

6. Describe the biggest challenge you anticipate when leading a team through social justice transformation. What strategies can you employ to address this challenge?

    _____
    _____
    _____
    _____

7. Consider your legacy as a leader. What impact do you hope to have on your team and/or organization in terms of social justice transformation?

    _____
    _____
    _____
    _____

Acknowledgements

I'd like to express my heartfelt gratitude to my family, whose unwavering support, patience, and encouragement have been the cornerstone of my journey to bring this book to life. You've inspired and sustained me through all the ups and downs, and I am eternally grateful for your belief in me. As I write this, every word was written with my son and unborn grandchildren in mind. Rhys, you are my inspiration – and the inspiration to so many. Your heart, mind, and soul are meant for greatness and I am honored that you chose me to be your mother.

I also extend my deepest thanks to those who, in various ways, encouraged me to put my thoughts on paper. Your words of motivation and belief in the importance of this work were a driving force behind my commitment to this project.

To those who questioned my abilities along the way, your doubt served as a powerful catalyst. It fueled my determination and reminded me of the significance of the message I wanted to share. Your doubt, especially when it came to my space in this work, showed me the power of societal privilege. As a white-presenting woman, I have been told I don't belong in the space of social justice. My work has shown the world that I belong – and I will continue to use my privileges to uplift the voices of those without that same privilege.

I owe a special debt of gratitude to my college professor, Dr. Ivy Goduka. Although I have been unable to locate you, your teachings kindled my curiosity and awakened me to the areas of privilege that I would later explore in this book. Your wisdom, kindness, and unwavering search for social justice, has been instrumental in my personal and intellectual journey, and I thank you for your guidance.

This book is a testament to the transformative power of community, mentorship, and personal growth, and I am profoundly thankful to all who have played a role in this endeavor. Your support, insights, and dedication have brought this work to fruition, and I am truly honored to share it with the world.

About the Author

Megan Fuciarelli is the proud Founder & CEO (Chief Empowerment Officer) of US² Consulting, a firm dedicated to provide a sense of belonging by empowering clients to be the CHANGE they wish to see in the world. As a retired Superintendent of schools, she spent much of her adult career in the educational realm. After growing up in Michigan and spending much of her adult life in the Chicago-land area, she returned back home to be closer to her parents. As an only child, her small family became a source of strength after having her son, Rhys. Since returning to Michigan, she spends much of her free time with her parents, cooking and traveling – two of the family loves. While her work is a passion for her, her commitment to changing the world through relationships is paramount.

Megan has earned multiple degrees and uses the information gained from all of them to help her run a successful business dedicated to helping the world ensure a sense of belonging. Her first degree, Bachelor of Science in Elementary Education, was earned from

Central Michigan University where she met the most impactful person on her social justice journey, Dr. Ivy Goduka from South Africa. After moving to Illinois, she went on to earn a Master of Arts in Teaching and Learning with an emphasis on Reading and a Master of Education in Educational Administration. She has also earned an ESL Endorsement and a certificate from Harvard in Urban School Leadership. She is also a certified Life Coach and Project Management Professional.

Throughout her career in social justice, she has worked with Learning for Justice, a project of Southern Poverty Law Center, International Institute for Restorative Practices, and partnered with Microsoft to co-create the "Anti-Racism Toolkit for Educators". She has been on multiple international stages, including the TEDx stage sharing, "When Implicit Bias Becomes Explicit". She has written for multiple publications and has been a guest on a variety of podcasts. Her career started in the PreK-12 education space and has expanded to the education of all humans – regardless of age, location, and sector.

Megan's legacy for the world is to release guilt, shame, and blame to reveal the inner CHANGEmaker in all of us. You are invited to learn more about her mission and offerings by clicking here: https://linktr. ee/us2consulting